The Corporation Illusion:
Unmasking 1871

Published April 9, 2024

ISBN 979-8-9901818-1-6

Printed In the United States of America

Table of Contents

Prologue

This book was interesting to write. I found myself experiencing different expressed-out-loud emotions. There were bouts of laughter, followed by interspersed moments of angry darts shooting out of my eyes while my fingers angrily typed, topics that sobered me to places of solemn angst, followed by more hold my stomach laughter, and ultimately copious amounts of protective righteous anger.

There is no part of me that is laughing at anyone unaware of what I am about to reveal. I've saved that for the ones who have subverted many. Those individuals can pound sand.

If you haven't gotten your hands on the companion book, "Patriot Psyop: The Battle For Your Mind," you're missing out! I bring it up because what you're about to dive into is a direct extension of the mind-bending ideas introduced there. The content here was just too explosive to cram into the first book.

Hold onto your hats, folks, because when it comes to the U.S. Corporation, you're in for a ride like no other! Get ready to have your mind blown by revelations so shocking, you'll wonder how you've never heard them before.

The Deep Dark of Early America

We are about to step together into a story that has captivated the hearts and minds of many, and possibly even you—an intriguing narrative woven into the murky fabric of American history. It's the story of an era gone by centered around the year 1871, a year when some believe the United States underwent a remarkable transformation, evolving from a sovereign nation to a corporation. This possibly freedom-altering situation is just begging us to make sense of it all. These chapters ahead dig deep and unearth the truth behind this fascinating and intriguing twist in America's journey inviting discovery where history's mysteries are revealed and the truth shines brightly.

It's the year 1776. Most American's perception is that in 1776 we won the Revolutionary War. Not so. This is when it began. In the middle of the war, the founders set about to craft what became our initial Constitution called the Articles of Confederation. The Articles were written in 1777 and ratified by all 13 colonies-turned-states in 1781 before the war was even over. Now that is some serious confidence! The war was not officially won until 1783 with the signing of the Treaty of Paris.

The war had been bravely fought and won with the individual militia of each colony brought together to form the Continental Army along with two other military forces created just to throw off Britain. Lafayette and the French also came to bear against the Brits, aiding us to our victory.

Before this, as the oppressed colonies prepared to throw off this encumbrance, The Continental Congress was established in 1774 with a very specific purpose: to devise a strategy for challenging British rule and securing independence. Central to their plan was the utilization of the existing colonial militia as the foundation for their military efforts. Additionally, Congress created both the Continental Marines and the Continental Navy as vital components of their strategy for success.

The Declaration of Independence written on July 4, 1776, formally declared the American colonies to be independent states, no longer under British rule. This marked the beginning of the process that eventually led to the recognition of these states as sovereign entities. The war officially concluded on September 3, 1783, with the signing of the Treaty of Paris. The process of statehood continued through the Revolutionary War and culminated in the ratification of the Articles of Confederation that same year, which established the initial framework for America's first federal government.

But now that independence had been achieved the purse was empty and we were owing. There were no funds to maintain a military, hence at the end of the war, the Continental Marines and Navy were disbanded by Congress. By June 2, 1784, all had been sent home except for two companies to safeguard military storehouses and armament. The next day, Congress voted that these men would form the first 1st American Regiment.

How does a nation function without a military? This was one of the shortcomings of the Articles. There was no funding set aside for a federal military presence. This, along with other glaring issues with the Articles set several of our founding fathers about the task of recrafting a better document.

During the Constitutional Convention, which took place in Philadelphia, Pennsylvania in May of 1787, James Madison, considered the "Father of the Constitution" along with Alexander Hamilton, George Washington, Benjamin Franklin, and others, recognized the weaknesses of the Articles of Confederation and sought to create a stronger and more effective system of government for the newly independent United States. To drum up interest in the new United States Constitution these men hoped to sell the states on, Alexander Hamilton, John Jay, and James Madison, set out to write the Federalist papers.

The Federalist Papers
The purpose of the Federalist Papers was to promote the ratification of the United States Constitution. They were a series of essays written under the pseudonym "Publius." The essays were published in newspapers and addressed various aspects of the proposed Constitution, including its structure, powers of government, and the principles behind it. The Federalist Papers are considered one of the most

important sources for understanding the intentions of the Founding Fathers in drafting the Constitution.

John wrote 5 essays, James wrote 29, and Alex wrote the other 51 in the span of six months! This was no small feat. These articles were what ultimately convinced the states to ratify what we now own as our sovereign document, The Constitution of the United States. The Constitution was ratified on June 21, 1788, when New Hampshire became the ninth state to ratify it, meeting the requirement for the Constitution to go into effect.

Not only did it fix several issues, but notably, it provided for a federal military. The militia that made up the army became the United States Army. A few years later the "Naval *Act* of 1794," authorized the construction of the first six ships for our newly formed U.S. Navy. The United States Marine Corps was formally established by Congress on July 11, 1798, by the "*Act* for Establishing a Marine Corps."

Let me just pause here to say how much I wish we could pause and dive deeper into all of these incredible aspects of our nation's beginning. I'm kind of hurrying through and hitting the highlights, but any of these fascinating topics that intrigue you, please follow your nose and discover more. We have been deprived of civics for far too long and should never have been without these basic understandings. I think we'd be in a different place today if this were required knowledge for all Americans.

Back to it, after the ratification of the Constitution, a deal was struck. The year was 1789, and the founders were contending over where the federal seat of power would be situated. Alexander Hamilton was the Secretary of the Treasury at that time. Hamilton, James Madison, and Thomas Jefferson met one evening over dinner to strike a deal; a quid pro quo. No one knows the details of that meeting, but we know that when the meeting concluded, Hamilton walked out of the room with the banks in New York, and James Madison and Thomas Jefferson walked out with the capitol along the Potomac just off of Virginia where they were from. Quoting the acclaimed play, *Hamilton*, written and produced by Lin-Manuel Miranda, "no one else was in the room where it happened."

This particular song from the play is intriguing to me and one of my favorites. One part of the lyrics go, "No one else really knows how the game is played, the art of the trade, How the sausage gets made. We just assume that it happens. But no one else is in the room where it happens."

I just find that fascinating. What deal did these men strike? I can tell you that they didn't turn the U.S. into a corporation. But this is the wrong century for that conversation.

(When I named this chapter, "The Deep Dark of Early America," I didn't mean dark as in nefarious. I meant dark as in unknown information. Now that our sleuthing lanterns are shining bright, let's dig deeper into the unillumined corners of these intriguing catacombs together.)

Pennsylvania Ave

B ack to the timeline, it is now 1790 and the building of the White House and other federal buildings is in the works. But before breaking ground, the land mass must be determined. The founders in charge concluded that the area for the federal seat would be no larger than 10 miles square, or, 100 square miles.

To give you a visual, picture a line 10 miles in length in one direction, connected by another wall by 10 miles. Build four of those into a square. Each distance of the area was 10 miles in length.

To carve out that space, Georgetown, a city of the state of Maryland, and the city of Alexandria belonging to Virginia were ceded (or given) by each of those states to create this 10 sq mile space. As well, not only were these two cities ceded but also other unpopulated land was given for the district by both states.

Picture with me a city called Georgetown, Maryland. It is no longer in existence today and we will cover that later, but at the time, Georgetown was a relatively small port town with a population of about 5000 people. Georgetown was incorporated as a city by an *ACT* of the Maryland General Assembly in accordance with state law in 1789 (I will explain "acts" later in the book). This type of incorporation granted Georgetown the status of a self-governing municipality with its own local government. But almost as soon as it had become its own incorporated municipality, it was given away by Maryland in the service of becoming the land for our nation's capitol.

The municipal incorporation of Georgetown provided the town with several benefits and powers, including:

1. Local Governance: Georgetown gained the ability to establish its own local government, including a mayor and city council, to manage local affairs and enact ordinances.

2. Taxation and Revenue: The city could levy taxes and collect revenue to fund public services and infrastructure projects within its jurisdiction.

3. Land Use Regulation: Georgetown could enact zoning laws and regulations to control land use and development within the city limits.

4. Public Services: The city could provide essential public services such as policing, firefighting, sanitation, and public education to its residents.

5. Legal Recognition: Municipal incorporation granted Georgetown legal recognition as a distinct entity with its own rights and responsibilities under Maryland law.

Overall, municipal incorporation empowered Georgetown to govern itself and meet the needs of its residents more effectively.

So, would that all end because it was given to the District of Columbia? No, the district founding architects thought it best for Georgetown to keep its current municipal incorporation intact. But instead of that incorporation being tied to the State of Maryland, it now folded up under the municipal governance of the District of Columbia. Same with Alexandria, Virginia.

Confused about incorporation? You won't be soon. Let's figure it out together, shall we?

Incorporation

This is where many become confused about the whole topic of "incorporation." There are different reasons to incorporate. In our day-to-day world, we think of incorporation as being the system used to create a private company. Unless you are in government and understand the other function of incorporating for the sake of a municipal government or you remember your civics class lessons about how your community, county, and state function, this thought process is a foreign one. This is where a good civics lesson comes in handy.

Incorporation, in the context of towns and cities, refers to the process by which a municipality is formally recognized as a legal entity by the state government. This recognition grants the municipality certain powers and responsibilities to govern itself and provide services to its residents in concert with the state.

When a town or city incorporates, it establishes a formal relationship with the state government, agreeing to abide by state laws and regulations while also gaining a degree of autonomy to manage its affairs. This relationship is often described as a form of "contract" between the municipality and the state, where the municipality agrees to certain obligations in exchange for the benefits of incorporation.

Some of the key aspects of incorporation include:

1. **Legal Status:** Incorporation gives the municipality legal standing as a distinct entity separate from the state government.

2. **Self-Governance:** Incorporated municipalities have the authority to establish their own local government, including a mayor, city council, and other officials, to make decisions on behalf of the community.

3. **Taxation and Revenue:** Incorporated municipalities can levy taxes, collect revenue, and manage their finances to fund local services and infrastructure.

4. **Services and Infrastructure:** Incorporated municipalities are responsible for providing essential services to residents, such as policing, firefighting, sanitation, and public works.

5. **Accountability:** Through incorporation, municipalities agree to comply with state laws and regulations and are accountable to the state government for their actions.

Overall, incorporation is a way for towns and cities to formalize their relationship with the state government, gain autonomy in local governance, and provide for the needs of their residents.

Municipal incorporation is the process by which a town or city becomes a self-governing entity, accountable to the state government, while private company incorporation is the process by which a business becomes a separate legal entity, accountable to its shareholders and governed by a board of directors.

You see that they are similar in how they function while being wildly different in purpose. A private business corporation may be set up as a nonprofit or for-profit. Very rarely there is a municipal for-profit incorporation. One well-known example of this is Disney World. It is established as a city, however, it is for profit, and thus, their municipality is formed corporately as a for-profit entity.

I grew up in the beautiful hills of the Ozarks in Southwest Missouri. If you've never been to one of the many scenic and fun destinations in that area you are missing out. Table Rock Lake is one of my favorite and most sacred childhood memories. Our family spent many a summer's day and night out on that gorgeous lake, surrounded by beautiful foliage and landscape. Nearby, the city of Branson, Missouri has been considered little Nashville. There are shows, events, theme parks, shops, and dining everywhere the eye can see. It is a city built on tourism and down-home country feels.

Nearby, the renowned theme park, Silver Dollar City, has been a several-generation pastime for our family. I live nowhere near there now, and yet we still find ways to get back there as often as possible. The whole park is set in the age of the Hatfields and McCoys and boasts all of the nostalgia of that era. You can watch an actual blacksmith create tools, watch a glass-blowing exhibition, partake of fresh-batch peanut brittle minutes after watching it being made and every employee the park over is dressed in period costumes, from cashiers in clothing stores to gunslingers in the streets putting on a show that is sure to delight. You can buy yourself a bonnet at any number of the mercantile stores and fit right in. There is even an undertaker walking around with a yardstick.

The roller coasters are arguably the envy of Missouri, and Six Flags and Worlds of Fun are both major theme parks in the state. I'd take the coasters at Silver Dollar City any day.

And guess what? The Silver Dollar is set up as its own incorporated municipality…for profit. But when you are talking about setting up a normal town, these are set up as nonprofit municipal entities, just as Georgetown and Alexandria were in their perspective states at the time they were given municipal autonomy. Your town is set up as a corporation as well unless you live in one of the rare cities that chose to go it alone without becoming incorporated or you live rurally.

Probably most of us have driven through the country at some time in life and seen the small communities that don't look big enough to be a town. I've seen this often, having driven all over the country. There will be a little nondescript sign that says "Unincorporated." Now you know why. The people there have not chosen to make an agreement with the state to be their own autonomous municipality. However, this does not mean they are without service. They still belong to a county. The county is responsible for infrastructure for any areas that are unincorporated within their borders.

Notably, unincorporated areas are not always small. In fact, The Woodlands, Texas is a large unincorporated area. And just as with the small areas, the county is the infrastructure for this area. The Woodlands sits in two different Texas counties, so both counties have areas of The Woodlands they are responsible for.

Why would The Woodlands opt for this and not become their own incorporated municipality?

The Woodlands, Texas, has chosen to remain unincorporated since its founding in 1974 for several reasons, including:

1. Taxes: Incorporating as a city would likely result in the imposition of additional taxes on residents and businesses. Remaining unincorporated allows The Woodlands to avoid these potential tax increases.

2. Services: The Woodlands receives a range of services, such as law enforcement, fire protection, and public works, from Montgomery County and Harris County. These services are generally satisfactory to residents, making incorporation less necessary.

3. Development: As an unincorporated community, The Woodlands has more flexibility in its development and land-use planning. This allows for more efficient growth and development strategies.

4. Costs: Incorporating as a city would bring additional costs, such as hiring municipal employees and establishing a city government. By remaining unincorporated, The Woodlands can avoid these costs.

Overall, the decision to remain unincorporated allows The Woodlands to maintain a high quality of life for its residents while avoiding some of the potential drawbacks of incorporation.

When referring back to our founding, these cities incorporated with their states as follows:

1. Boston, Massachusetts incorporated in 1822

2. New York City incorporated in 1898

3. Philadelphia incorporated in 1701

4. Charleston, South Carolina incorporated in 1783

So how does a municipal corporation come to exist?

Did you know that it is a decision made by the people who live in the area? That's right. It's the citizen's choice. How it comes about is different based on which state because everything runs through your state's unique constitution and laws.

In South Carolina, for instance, "Incorporation of a new municipality is accomplished by special election initiated by petition of 15 percent of electors and conducted by commissioners appointed by the Secretary of State pursuant to S.C. Code Title 5, Chapter 1, § 5- 1-10 through 5-1-110, and as amended in Act 77 effective July 1, 2005" (Municipal Association of South Carolina).

"Texas requires a standard form to be completed and filed with the county judge in the county in which the incorporation is to take place. Note that the application must be signed by at least 50 qualified voters who are residents in the community" (Quora).

Every state has its own laws about how a new municipality is formed, whether it's a city, township, or something else. But it's always in accordance with the will of the people living in the area.

Municipal corporations are not government overreach. They are a partnership the people choose to enter into with the state because they want to; Freedom-loving Americans doing the things that free people do because they can. Isn't that refreshing?

DC Inc.

Now that I have thoroughly bunny-trailed away from the founding of America and the creation of our capitol, it's time to come full circle and apply this information to the establishment of the District of Columbia.

We left off in 1790 when it was decided that the District of Columbia would be 10 miles sq or 100 square miles. It was even put into the Constitution that it may not exceed this size forever and ever amen. And it has not. In fact, it has gotten smaller. In 1824 Alexandria would be retroceded back to Virginia, leaving DC to remain to this current day 68.3 sq miles in total instead of 100 sq. miles. A seemingly unimportant piece of trivia, however, some have misinterpreted what is meant by 10 miles sq, not realizing that this equals 100 sq miles. Some thought this constitutional adherence had been usurped because the mental image is that it should only be 10 miles. Squaring things mathematically can be tricky. It's an understandable mistake. But it is also an easy one to rectify for anyone who is concerned. The District of Columbia is smaller than it could be constitutionally.

It was the Residence *ACT* of 1790 that authorized the creation of a new federal city along the Potomac River. Why is it a "federal City?" Because it answers to Congress, not a state.

What is an Act?

The use of "Acts" in the context of legislative documents and laws dates back to medieval England. The term "Act" was used to describe a formal written record of a decision or decree made by a governing body, such as a king or parliament. Over time, the term came to be used more specifically to refer to laws or statutes enacted by a legislative body.

In the United States, Congress is the legislative body responsible for passing acts that become federal law. This authority is granted to Congress by the U.S. Constitution, which establishes Congress as the national legislature and grants it the power to make laws. The Constitution also outlines the process by which laws are created, including the requirement that both the House of Representatives and the Senate must pass a bill before it can become law. The decision to grant Congress the authority to pass acts and make laws was made by the framers of the Constitution during the Constitutional Convention of 1787. They believed that a strong national legislature was necessary to govern effectively and to ensure that laws were uniform and applied consistently throughout the country.

Our founding fathers drew inspiration from England's governance but adapted these concepts into the rich fabric of a Constitutional Republic. They carefully omitted elements of British law that elevated the government above the people. While some practices were borrowed from British governance, they became uniquely American after securing our freedom, no longer under Britain's jurisdiction on American soil.

Setting up DC's Government Structure

So now what? They've picked the spot, and certainly, blueprints were being drawn up and contractors secured for the building of the most significant facilities ever to that point in history for this burgeoning nation. Remember that Alexander Hamilton negotiated for the banks to remain in New York and Madison and Jefferson got the capitol close to home. The next few years would be pivotal for our standing on the world stage for many reasons, but for the purposes of this book, we'll leave those elements for another day and stay on topic.

I will leave that there with this caveat. I do not personally love what Alexander Hamilton did financially during this time. He was the treasury secretary chosen by George Washington, and he was given carte blanche access to establish America's banking system, including establishing national credit, at the expense of the states, to prop up federal banking power.

What I want you, my readers, to realize, is that THIS factor right here is the piece where I believe our country went down a dangerous path, giving banking way too much power over the people.

But let's step away from the banking system for the sake of getting back on topic and fast forward a few years to the year 1801. It was in this year that The District of Columbia formally became an entity. Let's talk this through. We already know where Georgetown and Alexandria came from. But that is not all. Not only did Maryland give Georgetown and Virginia give Alexandria, both states also gave undeveloped and unincorporated land.

(Ultimately, all of the land our capitol sits upon today was once part of the state of Maryland because not only was Alexandria retroceded, but so was all the land Virginia initially gave for the District.)

Congress established the District of Columbia by passing the Act of the District of Columbia, (or as we learned earlier, enacting legislation) making it the new federal seat for the United States of America. Between 1790 and 1801, the area outside of Georgetown and Alexandria saw significant growth as people settled there, turning the undeveloped land into homesteads and communities. The population boomed thanks to contractors, government workers, and others moving in. This influx necessitated the development of infrastructure like roads and buildings to support the growing city. Incorporation became crucial, as it is the pathway by which the governing body (Congress) can provide for the city's needs, with residents agreeing to their part of the deal.

The establishment of a new city, Washington City, (formed in what was initially an uninhabited portion formerly belonging to the state of Maryland but now was being settled) and the creation of the new Federal District of Columbia were both established in the same act, known as the Organic Act of 1801. This act officially incorporated the cities of Washington and Georgetown into the District of Columbia and placed the entire district under the exclusive jurisdiction of Congress. All of our territories come under the

19

headship of Congress. It also provided for the organization of a local government for the district. At this time Alexandria was still part of DC, however, they were under their own incorporation also flowing up under the District of Columbia and no longer under Virginia. So now you have an area that has 2 separate municipal incorporations, meaning two different governance infrastructures, to support and partner with the people living within the now-established District of Columbia.

Within 6 years, there were growing pangs, and once again, this act had shortcomings that needed to be addressed. We saw this with the Articles of Confederation. On this much smaller scale, change was needed. Congress went back to the drawing board in 1807 and revised the Act, coming up with the Revised Organic Act of 1807.

This Act was passed to address the shortcomings that had arisen since the passage of the original one. Some of the key reasons for the passage of the 1807 Act include:

1. Governance: The original Organic Act of 1801 established a complicated system of government for the District of Columbia that was seen as inefficient and cumbersome. The 1807 act reorganized the local government structure, creating a more streamlined and effective system.

2. Elections: The original act had no provisions for the appointment of local officials. Instead, it allowed for the appointment of officials by the President of the United States, which was seen as undemocratic because it did not give residents of the district a direct voice in their government. The 1807 act introduced provisions for the election of local officials, giving residents of the district more control over their government.

3. Representation: The residents of the District of Columbia were not represented in Congress, which was seen as unfair taxation without representation. The 1807 act did not grant full congressional representation to the district, but it did provide for the election of a delegate to the House of Representatives, giving residents some voice in Congress.

Overall, the Organic Act of 1807 was passed to improve the governance and representation of the District of Columbia.

Please notice that in every instance an act is mentioned it is an ACTion done for the states, territories, and country of the United States of America, for Americans, and enacted by Congress. At no time have you seen an act in any of the history that I have walked you through ever used as an instrument that negotiated any dealings or settled any disputes or created any laws or borders for or with any other countries outside of the U.S. And they never do. You can research every act that has ever been enacted and you will find that no act ever communicates or makes deals with other countries.

Post Civil War

Years go by. Lots of things occur. The country continues to establish new states, and each state signs on to accept the terms of the Constitution of the United States while also creating their own state constitutions.

In the 1860s America finds itself in crisis. The country is divided and war breaks out. Surviving the meltdown, you can likely imagine lots of shifting and growth occurred within this 100 sq miles since the early 1800s when the original governmental infrastructure was established for DC. A major shift in population had developed over time.

The land that had been given by Maryland was now bursting at the seams post-Civil War. Many more people have moved into the area. The current Revised Act of 1807 once again is found to be wanting as far as being able to attend to the needs of large-scale growth. the governance structure created by the 1807 Act proved inadequate, and there were ongoing issues with the administration and management of the district.

The Organic Act of 1871 was intended to address these issues by further reorganizing and modernizing the governance of the District of Columbia. While the 1807 act had established a single municipality there were still separate charters for Georgetown and Washington City. The 1871 act made additional changes to the governance structure, including the establishment of a governor, a board of commissioners, both selected by the president, and a legislative assembly elected by the residents for the district. It also revoked the individual charters of the cities of Washington and Georgetown, consolidating them into the new District of Columbia government. So now instead of having separate mayors, councils, and other officials, it was consolidated into one system for the whole area. The goal was to create a more efficient and robust system for the bursting metropolis.

There is so much to unpack about the Civil War. I wish this book could cover those intricacies, but as this book is a companion to "Patriot Psyop: The Battle For Your Mind" I will do my best to not bunny trail into incredibly interesting "other" topics for the sake of your generosity and time you are investing in this information.

But also...turn the page!

Time Travel to 1871

I have a great idea. Instead of me telling you about 1871, how much more fun would it be if we travel back in time and take in the views of early America on the street level? This is a captivating peek into what life was like during the infancy stages of our beautiful America. Presenting this epic zoom into history is James H Whyte. Sit back and enjoy this trip down the streets of DC.

"I deeply appreciate the honor which this society has accorded to me a relatively junior member and a resident of Washington for a mere fifteen years by inviting me to give this address. Let me say at the outset that I am by training no professional historian, and that my approach to the subject of this paper: "The District of Columbia Territorial Government", may strike you accordingly as somewhat unorthodox.

As a citizen who is deeply concerned with the question of civic participation in local government, I have for some years been particularly interested in that period following the Civil War in which all classes of District residents voted to elect their municipal representatives. I have studied not only the standard texts of such writers as William Tindall, W. B. Bryan, Dr. Schmeck-ebier and others, but have also made a point of examining every newspaper, pamphlet letter and manuscript in the Library of Congress, the National Archives and in the possession of this society which might shed additional light upon the period. I sincerely hope that the result of these investigations may prove interesting to you this evening and that they may further stimulate a closer examination by the citizens of the District of so important a phase of local history.

Let me start this evening by rolling back the curtain of time to the 20th of February in the year 1871. Washington is celebrating the paving of Pennsylvania Avenue by a three-day carnival. The schools are out on holiday, and more than 10,000 visitors have flocked to the city. From the Capitol grounds to the Treasury building the Avenue is lined with spectators. On both sides of the street buildings are adorned with pictures, streamers and evergreens, and the conspicuously new wooden pavement stretches from curb to curb like a ballroom floor. Foot races are on the program, and horse races of all kinds, from six-in-hands to dog carts. At night calcium burners, gas jets and Chinese lanterns illuminate the streets, and fireworks are touched off at the Treasury portico. The new Corcoran Gallery at the corner of Pennsylvania Avenue and 17th Street is the scene of the most brilliant ball that Washington has ever witnessed.

The celebrations continue through the next day, Shrove Tuesday.

There is a masquerade procession along the Avenue, more displays of fireworks and two masked balls. On the following day at the new Arlington Hotel across from the White House the Mayor and City Council of Washington hold a banquet for the press and prominent visitors to the capital, and the great Carnival comes to a close.

All this civic effervescence is meant to celebrate much more than the mere paving of Washington's principal thoroughfare. Congress on February 21st has passed a bill providing for a new District government, which the citizens all believe is to usher in a new and more prosperous era for the residents of the national capital. In order to appreciate their sentiments, let me briefly review the course of municipal affairs in Washington since the end of the Civil War.

In appearance the city has changed very little since 1865. Apart from the White House and Capitol there are hardly any government buildings of importance to be seen, only the Treasury, Patent Office, Post Office and Smithsonian Institute. The Potomac comes almost to the foot of the White House, and the Washington Monument still lies uncompleted for lack of funds. The northern limit of Washington City is still Boundary Street (Florida Avenue), and above it lie but a handful of scattered farms. To the West is the separate municipality of Georgetown, linked by one ancient wooden bridge across Rock Creek at M Street.

Since L'Enfant's plan called for avenues far wider than those of any other American city, Washington taxpayers have been unable to afford the money required to pave them, and Congress has up till now been-extremely niggardly in its appropriations.

The water supply is inadequate for the population, which has increased since the war by 100%, only a few of the streets are lit by gas, and the old Canal back of the Avenue is still an eyesore and stinking disgrace. Things have changed little since 1867 when Henry Latham, an English visitor, wrote, "To make a Washington street take one marble temple or public office, a dozen good houses of brick and a dozen of wood, and fill in with sheds and fields. Some blight seems to have fallen on this city. It is the only place we have seen which is not full of growth and vitality".

The great difference between Washington before and after the War is in the nature of its population. In 1860, according to the Census, there were only 14,296 Negroes in the District, of whom over 11,000 were free. Some of them, such as the caterers James Wormley and John Gray, were men of means; the free colored population has established its own churches and provided a large number of private schools for its children.

Except during the Snow Riots of 1835 there had been little race friction for many years, even though prejudice unquestionably existed, and many residents of Washington and Georgetown had been openly sympathetic to the Southern cause. The War, however, had brought to the District more than 30,000 Negro refugees, chiefly from the plantations of Virginia and Maryland, and soldiers who had been mustered out there at the close of the fighting. Some of the Negroes lived in abandoned fortifications, others in miserable alley shacks; thousands jammed together in areas with such revealing names as Murder Bay, Foggy Bottom, Swampdoodle and Vinegar Hill.

There was little work for the refugees; their health conditions were shocking, and a menace to those of the entire community. Congress had made several appropriations for their relief, but it had thrown a heavy burden upon the taxpayers of the District by appropriating a portion of the public school fund for the education of colored children.

Mayor Richard Wallach had accurately expressed the sentiments of the older residents when he refused to hand over the colored school funds, on the ground that Congress had been unfair to Washington taxpayers to saddle the community with this expense, since the refugees were likely to contribute nothing in taxes and to remain a public liability for many years.

However, congress had been more disposed to grant political rights to the colored population of the District than to provide it with a livelihood. In the minds of such leaders of the Republican Party as Charles Sumner, the enfranchisement of the Negroes in the District was to be the first step in a comprehensive plan for Negro suffrage in all the Southern states. In January 1867, Congress had passed over Andrew Johnson's veto a Bill granting equal suffrage to the colored men of the District in spite of the

27

*overwhelming opposition of the white population in Washington
and Georgetown.*

*In 1868 Sayles J. Bowen, a Radical Republican, had been
elected Mayor by the narrow margin of 83 votes. Bowen was a
man of upright character, whom Lincoln had appointed
Postmaster of Washington during the War. He had the full
support of the colored voters and also of all Republicans,
including the three daily news-papers, the Evening Star,
National Republican and Chronicle. Bowen had endeavored to
make a start with improving the streets but, not wishing to raise
property taxes, made but few paving contracts during his first
year in office. However in 1869 the municipal elections had
given Bowen an overwhelming majority, and the Democrats had
been almost completely ousted from both city councils.*

*One-third of the members of the Board of Common Councils to
be elected were Negroes, and other colored men received
important civic positions. Bowen furthermore revealed his true
position in his inaugural message to the councils, when he openly
advocated the integration of the white and colored school systems.
At this point many of his Republican supporters began to be
alarmed, and some of them began to seek methods to eliminate
Bowen from the political scene.*

*Among the Republican politicians of Washington, the natural
leader was Alexander Shepherd. Born in 1835, Shepherd had
been left an orphan at the age of 12. Within a few years he had
become a partner in the gas fitting business of John W.
Thompson, the most flourishing plumber in the city. In 1861
Shepherd enlisted as a private in the Union Army and had a
year later been elected to the Board of Common Council.
Physically Shepherd was a large man, weighing more than 200
pounds, and over six feet tall. His hair was brown, his eyes blue,
his chin that of a fighter. William Tindall, his secretary,
remarked many years later, "I have never heard another male
voice that was equal to his in richness and fullness of tone as an*

28

instrument of conversation". In 1865 Shepherd was elected Secretary to the newly-formed Board of Trade, and through his friendship with the banker, Henry D. Cooke, became acquainted with General Ulysses Grant. Politically Shepherd was a Republican, but not a doctrinaire nor a Radical. He was not hostile to the Negroes, but he objected as a taxpayer to their becoming a permanent municipal charge.

No man was more passionately concerned than he with the improvement of the national capital, and he had long held the view that the Federal Government, as the largest owner of property in the District, should make a far larger contribution to its upkeep. In 1870 he had signed a memorial to the Senate District Committee, petitioning Congress to make use of the unemployed Negroes for the paving of Washington streets and other public works.

Shepherd at first supported the Bowen administration through the Evening Star, in which he had at that time a quarter interest, but had turned against Bowen when it appeared clear that he was unable to handle the situation competently. Bowen lacked the hard-boiled political experience to resolve the conflicting claims of the ward commissioners, and he was obliged to spread the work of improvements over different areas of the city in order to retain his influence with the voters. As a result much gravelling and grading had been performed, but very little paving, and yet the floating debt of the Corporation (local government charter) had soared. By January, 1870, the city's financial state had become so grave that the furniture of the Mayor's office had been seized in a judgment granted against the municipality.

This incident had served to fan into flame the smoldering public dissatisfaction with the Bowen administration. At a meeting of influential Washington citizens, held in the real estate offices of Kilborn and Latta, Shepherd expressed his opinion that the only way to solve the recurrent financial crises was to unify the local administrations of the District, and to provide for increased participation by the Federal government. Two days later he presented to Congress a draft Bill endorsed by the Citizens' Committee which provided for a modified form of Territorial administration. A Governor and Legislative Council for the District was to be appointed by the Executive, and a House of Assembly of 25 members was to be elected with legislative powers equivalent to those which had been conferred by charter upon Washington and Georgetown. The District was to be represented in Congress by an elected Delegate.

However, Congress was to retain its traditionally exclusive power over the District, including the right to repeal any legislation passed by the new government.

In the election campaign of June 1870 all the Washington newspapers except the Radical Chronicle came out against Mayor Bowen, who was standing for re-election. The opposition Republicans united with the Democrats behind a so-called "Reform" candidate, Matthew G. Emery. Emery was strongly supported by Shepherd, who was convinced that Washington could expect no larger appropriations from Congress if Bowen were to be re-elected. Crosby Noyes, in the Evening Star, made strong appeals to the colored voters, who held the balance of power. Many of them, who had worked for the Corporation as day laborers, had not been paid for weeks, and the Star claimed that other colored men had been imported into Washington from nearby Maryland and Virginia to vote for Bowen. The campaign against the Mayor, who was compared with the infamous Boss Tweed of New York, was one of unparalleled abuse. The turn out of voters was large, and Bowen was defeated by more than 3000 votes. Only four of his supporters were elected to the Common Council and two to the Board of Aldermen.

During the administration of Mayor Emery, who concerned himself with putting the financial affairs of the Corporation (local infrastructure) in order, Shepherd and his friends had devoted themselves to lobbying for the Territorial Bill. Shepherd had become a close friend of President Grant, who was deeply concerned in the improvement of the national capital and used his influence with leaders in Congress to help promote the Bill. In February 1871 the head of the House District Committee, Rep. Burton C. Cook of Illinois introduced a measure for a change of District administration which closely followed the proposal of Shepherd and the Citizens' Committee in 1870.

The theory of the Territorial Bill, its author explained, was to secure a conservative influence in the District administration by the appointment of its chief officers by the Federal Government. The Bill actually represented a half-way stage to the commission form of government which Senator Morrill had proposed in 1865, and the Cook Bill provided for considerably less authority for District officials than that of other Territorial administrations. The executive was to appoint the Governor, a Legislative Council of eleven members, and a five-man Board of Health. In addition there was to be created a Board of Public Works consisting of five members, also presidential appointees. The only elective offices were the 22 members

of the House of Delegates (the District had been divided anew to make provision for Georgetown and the County of Washington) and a Delegate to Congress. In Section 18 of the Bill it was stated that "nothing shall be construed to deprive Congress of the power of legislation over said District in as ample manner as if this law had not been enacted".

A limit was placed upon the amount of money which the Territorial Government was permitted to borrow-5% of the assessed value of real property in the District-and such a loan had to be ratified by both Councils and the Governor.

It is impossible to know for the lack of documentary evidence whether Shepherd was responsible for the section of the Act

*which created the Board of Public Works. The original bill
which he and the Citizens' Committee had drafted contained no
such provision.*

*Similar Boards did, however, exist in other American cities at
this time had been responsible for a vast campaign of civic
improvements which had cut huge avenues across ancient streets
and transformed the old city into a modern metropolis. The
District Board was subject to a number of restrictions; although
it was given exclusive authority over the streets, sewers etc. and
the power to disburse money collected from taxpayers for
improvements.*

*Contracts were not to be awarded or payments made unless
sanctioned by the Legislature, and any contract in which a
member of the Board had a personal interest was to be voided.
In theory the Bill provided sufficient legislative safeguards,
according to the traditional American theory of checks and
balances, however differently matters turned out to be in practice.*

*The majority of District residents, including members of the
Board of Trade, heartily endorsed the Territorial Bill, which
President Grant signed on February 21st, 1871, the date of the
Washington Carnival.*

*However in March, when the presidential appointments to the
new District government were announced, the Democrats were
highly disturbed. Henry D. Cooke, brother of the Republican
banker, Jay Cooke, and head of the First National Bank of
Washington, was named Governor, and Shepherd Vice-
President of the Board of Public Works. Others appointed to
the Board were A. B. Mullett, Architect to the Treasury, S. P.
Brown, a contractor and real estate speculator and James
Magruder, an Army engineer.*

*The large property owners, most of whom were Democrats, were
bitterly resentful of the partisan nature of the appointments.*

'Not one old resident, nor a Democrat, nor a Catholic nor an Irishman', complained the Georgetown Courier, 'yet we have three darkies, Douglass, Gray and Hall, a German, two natives of Maine and one of Massachusetts'. The President's nominee as Secretary of the District, General Norton P. Chipman, was chosen as candidate for District Delegate on the Republican ticket. Chipman was a practicing patent attorney, an excellent speaker, who had many influential friends in Congress.

In the elections of April, 1871, Chipman was elected by more than a 4000 majority and 15 Republicans returned to the House of Delegates, two of them Negroes. Many colored men also received clerical positions in the new government and with the Board of Public Works. The Democrats, who had hoped that the Territorial administration would eliminate the colored office-holders, were bitterly disappointed with the election results, and they claimed through their organ, The Patriot, that the elections had been fraudulent. Since Democrats had been excluded from the Legislative Council and were politically impotent, they felt compelled to oppose any scheme which the new government would suggest.

It was not long before the opposition found its target. In June, 1871, three weeks after the Territorial administration had been inaugurated, the Board of Public Works announced its 'comprehensive plan of improvements', which was conceived on a heroic scale. The original plan of Major L'Enfant, which for decades had remained a dream, was at last to be realized. The grading of the principal streets and avenues was to be made uniform, in order to make possible the magnificent vistas called for in the original city plan. The streets were to be paved in a variety of materials stone,

concrete, macadam and wood and the widest avenues were to be planted with trees and gardens planted by the property owners in front of their houses. This would reduce the width of the area to

33

be paved and render the cost less expensive. The Tiber Creek was to be arched over and to become the principal sewer of the District, draining the waters of northwest Washington and Georgetown into the Potomac. Many new miles of sewerage were to be constructed to take care of the present and future requirements of the city. The

plan called for a system of fixed prices to be established by the Board, which would serve as a basis for contracts; it was claimed that this feature would prove more satisfactory than taking bids from contractors or paying laborers by the day, as had been done in the past. The cost of these improvements was estimated to be $6,000,000.00, of which one-third was to be paid by the owners of property to be improved and the balance, $4,000,000.00, to be raised by a bond issue.

The large property owners in the District lost little time after the plan had been approved by the Legislature to organize in opposition against it. They contended that the existed funded debt of the corporations and county amounted to over $3,000,000.00 and that, since the total amount of assessed property in the District was only $77,000,000.00, it would not be possible to increase the debt limit without exceeding the 5% limit fixed by the Organic Act. It would furthermore be necessary to hold a special election to ratify the loan.

On August 2nd Justice Wylie of the District Supreme Court granted an injunction against the Board, and the District government was obliged to make arrangements for a special election. On November 11th Chief Justice Carter reversed the injunction verdict, and a few days later the elections were held. The loan was endorsed by the sweeping majority of 2,748 to 1202, and the Republicans won 20 out of the 22 seats in the House of Delegates. There was now no legal obstacle to the execution or the improvements, and immediately laborers started in every part of the city tearing up streets.

34

The method in which the improvements were carried out proved very difficult for the residents of Washington to endure. 'It was a daily occurrence', wrote E. E. Barton in 'Washington City', for citizens to leave their houses in the morning as usual, and when they returned in the evening the sidewalks and curbs, which not infrequently had been but recently laid down at their own expense, all torn up and carted away. The established grades of the streets were changed, some filled up and others cut down, leaving houses perched up on banks 20 feet high. while others were covered nearly to the roof. Not infrequently buildings had their foundations so injured that they were in danger of falling, and owners were notified to render them safe in 30 days, or they would be pulled down.

The contractors often displayed great indifference towards the feelings of property owners. Once a contract had been awarded them by the Board, many felt impelled to stake their claim immediately by tearing up a street, even though they realized that it would be months before they would be able to complete the work. The unusually cold winter of 1872-3 and the outbreak of epizootic, or horse disease, still further slowed up the progress of the improvements.

Public opinion was irked by the supposed favoritism of the Board towards such important men as Senators Edmunds of Vermont and Bayard of Delaware, whose adjoining houses on Massachusetts Avenue had been left perched in the air by the new grade, and to Justice Wylie, whose house at Thomas Circle was moved at the expense of the Board. These men had been granted tax relief, while, small property owners were often obliged to sell when unable to borrow money to pay the heavy assessments.

In January, 1872, following a memorial to Congress signed by 1000 property owners, the House of Representatives appointed an Investigating Committee to examine District affairs. Some members of the opposition had charged that Shepherd, who

35

owned considerable property in the northwest section of Washington, had cut down the grades of streets in order to improve his own investments. It was claimed that Shepherd, together with Governor Cooke and Hallett Kilbourn, had formed a real estate pool, and that they were buying up real estate in sections which were to be improved immediately.

No definite proof of these allegations, however, could be established, and Shepherd emerged from the investigation with flying colors. The Democrats had also hoped that the investigation would reveal charges of illegal voting by Negroes, but even the editor of the Patriot, the leading opposition newspaper, when placed on the witness stand, was unable to substantiate his charges. The report of the Committee, which appeared on May 14th, sustained the action of the Board with but few reservations. 'The authorities had become somewhat intoxicated with the spirit of improvement', the Report stated, and added that 'care was not taken to have strict economy prevail in every department'. However, Shepherd and other members of the Board were cleared of all charges of personal profit, and they were commended for their zeal, energy and wisdom.

The two Democrats of the Committee, John M. Crebs and Robert B. Roosevelt, signed a minority report, which complained of the excessive expenditures of the Board and called for making all officers of the District government elective except that of Governor.

All members of the Board, in their opinion, should be required to place bond and be placed directly under legislative control, and the Board should issue warrants upon the District Treasury instead of issuing independent checks.

Shepherd had triumphed, but his problems were by no means solved. Before Congress adjourned it set a limit of $10,000,000.00 upon the amount which the District might

36

borrow, including in this figure the old funded debt of the corporations and county, which amounted to over $4,000,000.00. Since all but $500,000.00 of the $4,000,000.00 had been expended, there was left only $1,000,000.00 with which to complete the improvements.

Nevertheless Shepherd, feeling that the majority of citizens supported him, continued his plans undaunted. On the evening of September 3rd the old Northern Liberties Market on the site of the Central Public Library, long an unsanitary eyesore, was removed over the heads of the market men; Shepherd had taken the precaution of inviting to dinner at his farm the only Justice of the District Supreme Court in the city who might have granted an injunction. One of the butchers was killed in the demolition, and public sentiment against Shepherd flared up so violently that he was obliged to leave his office under an armed guard.

On November 18th, after Grant had been re-elected President and the Patriot had folded, he pulled off still another coup. This time a force of 200 laborers pulled up a section of track belonging to the Baltimore and Ohio Railroad which passed directly at the foot of Capitol Hill, which had long formed a serious traffic hazard. For the first time Shepherd was in absolute power; the recent District elections had again brought a Republican landslide in the House, and Chipman was re-elected Delegate. The Governor was a mild man, who never questioned his intentions, and the commissioner of Public Buildings and Grounds, General Babcock, was an intimate friend.

Shepherd moved in the fall to a magnificent mansion at the corner of Connecticut Avenue and K Street, which had cost him $50,000; he already owned a large farm in the county, he was happily married, the father of a large and growing family.

In spite of his local successes, however, Shepherd was becoming one of the favorite targets of the opposition press outside of Washington. The newspapers which had backed Greeley in the national election of 1872 were united in their abuse of the District government. Pamphlets were published in Washington ridiculing the Board and complaining of the high cost of the Territorial administration. Robert Roosevelt, who had become the chief spokesman for the Democrats and District property owners, made several speeches in the House attacking the extravagance of the Board, and claiming that the Federal Government had been defrauded by dishonest measurements made by District surveyors for work done on Federal property.

Roosevelt, as one of the Citizens' Committee responsible for the defeat of Boss Tweed in New York, lost no opportunity to press the parallel between Tweed and Shepherd.

In spite of these attacks in Congress the administration dealt very generously with their District appropriations. In 1872 and 1873 $3,250,000.00 were allocated to the Territorial government to cover the cost of improvements on Federal property.

The generosity of Congress produced, however, some unexpected results; many hard-pressed property owners delayed paying their assessments in the hope that still further appropriations would be forthcoming, and taxpayers all over the nation were hence forward to pay considerably more attention to the financial state of the District, in which for the first time they held so large a stake.

By the beginning of 1873 the Territorial Government was feeling the pinch. The cost of the improvements was proving to be greater than the Board had believed possible even with the generous appropriations of Congress. Certificates of indebtedness bearing interest had to be issued to property owners for work which had not yet been completed. A sewer tax was introduced, which hit particularly hard those dwelling in the swampy eastern sections of the city. The property tax in Washington was raised to $2.00, the legal maximum, and in the county to $1.50. In

May 1873 S. P. Brown was replaced on the Board by Henry Willard, the hotel keeper, as a move to placate the business interests of the community.

But the financial miracle for which Shepherd hoped never happened. Instead came the crash of Jay Cooke in September, the closing of the First National Bank of Washington, and Henry Cooke's resignation as Governor. Although Shepherd was immediately appointed in his place and quickly confirmed by the Senate he had become an even more conspicuous target for the opposition press. Such papers as the New York Herald, Tribune, Sun and World lost no opportunity to attack the District 'Ring', and Washington financial affairs were now front-page news. He could still, of course, count on the loyalty of the President, and the Washington press was unanimously behind him.

In December, 1873, the Board of Public Works published the achievements of the past two years: 58½ miles of wooden pavement laid, 28½ miles of concrete, 93 of macadam, gravel and block, 208 miles of sidewalk, 127 miles of sewers, 6,000 trees planted.

Washington was now the best-lit and best-paved city in the United States and its water supply was more plentiful than that of New York. A few days later the President, in his message to Congress, paid high tribute to the Board for its accomplishments, and again asked for generous appropriations for the forthcoming fiscal year.

However the situation at the end of 1873 was vastly different from what it had been a year before. The financial crash of September had shaken the nation; unemployment was widespread, and retrenchment the order of the day. Moreover the past year had exposed the operations of the Credit Mobilier in which leading Republicans in Congress had been implicated, and other revelations had made party leaders particularly sensitive to charges of corruption.

Following another memorial by property owners Congress appointed a joint committee of members from both Houses to examine a second time the conduct of the District government, and especially of the Board of Public Works.

Time does not permit me this evening to devote to the investigation of 1874, which lasted for three months, and the report of which consumes three volumes of 1000 pages each. the attention which it deserves. It is sufficient to summarize the findings of the Report, which disclosed that many of the business methods employed by the Board were highly irregular. The system of fixed prices was condemned as leading to favoritism in the allocation of contracts.

Faulty measurements had been made for work done on behalf of the Federal government. While Shepherd was not personally mentioned, the Board was condemned for permitting him to exercise such unlimited control. The vouchers of the Board's treasurer were found not to correspond with his payments and the auditor of the Board had no book by which the certificates of indebtedness could be checked. The sewer tax and the certificates were burdens, the Report stated which violated the spirit, if not the letter, of the Organic Act.

The floating debt of the District, together with the funded debt, was estimated to exceed $18,000,000.00, $8,000,000.00 more than the limit authorized by Congress. The Committee considered that the Territorial form of government had been too cumbrous and expensive, and that a temporary form of administration should be devised until Congress should have time to consider a permanent solution.

Shortly before the Joint Committee had issued its report, its members agreed upon a Bill for a commission form of

40

government for the District. The councils and all elected offices were to be abolished, and Army engineers were to take over the public works program.

The floating debt of the District was to be examined by the United States Treasury, and Sinking Fund Commissioners appointed to fund the debt over a 50-year period. Property taxes were temporarily to be raised to $3.00 in Washington, $2.50 in Georgetown and $2.00 in the County, and salaries of all District officers were to be cut by 20%. The Bill was signed by President Grant on June 21st, when the Councils adjourned for the last time.

Fired by sentiment and a passion for souvenirs somewhat unique in a legislative body, some of the members of the House of Delegates removed inkwells, desks and chairs from the Council chamber; one of them, who concealed a duster in his trouser leg, was to give to the last session of an elected government in the District the nickname of 'Feather Duster Legislature'.

In reviewing the history of the Territorial Government two factors must be considered which the Joint Committee doubtless felt were too politically explosive to mention. In the first place, the system of checks and balances established by the Act of 1871 had been nullified by the appointment of an exclusively Republican Legislative Council by President Grant. There was no opposition within the District government capable of constructive criticism. This lack of opposition encouraged Shepherd in his autocratic policy; instead of spreading the improvements over a longer period of time, he was led to attempt all within the short space of two years. The inescapable conclusions are that Shepherd realized that the Federal Government would be forced to save the government of the national capital from bankruptcy and that the ultimate form of administration of the District was a matter of lesser importance to him than the completion of the improvements as planned.

41

The question of Negro suffrage, which was avoided in the Report must also be mentioned, especially since this remains today the chief obstacle to District Home rule. It seems significant to me that the chief outcries made by Democrats of illegal voting by Negroes were after municipal elections in which they had been defeated; in 1870, on the other hand, when Negro voters had helped to defeat Bowen, no such accusations were heard. Neither the 1872 nor the 1874 investigations revealed that Negroes had voted illegally, although evidence disclosed pressure upon laborers by contractors who were employed by the Board of Public Works.

The Negroes were not, however, the only large racial group employed as laborers; the Irish, who were almost as numerous, and many of whom were equally illiterate, were as united in their support of the Board as the Negroes. In 1873, when the pressure of the special assessments became too great for the small property owners to bear, it was a Negro member of the Legislative Council, John Gray, who introduced a law permitting the payment of the assessments in four installments, which was subsequently adopted by the District government.

The position of Shepherd at the close of the investigation was an ambiguous one, although the report had made no accusation of his using public money for his own advantage, the Senate nevertheless had refused to confirm his appointment as Commissioner by a vote of 36 to 4. He could doubtless draw some consolation from the Poland Judiciary Committee Report published on June 5th, which substantiated his contention that the Federal Government should make a larger contribution to the District budget. 'There is something revolting to a proper sense of justice', the Report stated, 'in the idea that the United States should hold free from taxation more than half the area of the capital city, should require to be maintained a city upon an unusually expensive scale from which the ordinary revenues derived from commerce and manufacture are excluded; that in such a case the burden of maintaining the expenses for the capital should fall upon the resident population'. Contrary to the expectations of his enemies, Shepherd remained in Washington for several more years, looking after his manifold business interests and lobbying in Congress for further District appropriations.

In 1877 Shepherd had the satisfaction of seeing the same figures that he had produced during the 1874 Investigation incorporated in a memorial that a non-partisan Citizens' Committee presented to the Senate. These figures, which showed the value of the Federal Government property in the District, and the area occupied by streets and avenues, were used as the basis for the Committee's claim that Congress should provide in the District Government Bill under consideration for one-half of the expenses of running the District. The 50-50 provision which was subsequently incorporated into the Organic Act of 1878 was unquestionably the result of Shepherd's long fight for his native city. If one takes a long view of the situation, the economic benefits that the District derived for more than forty years from 1878 to 1925 as a result of the financial assistance of the Federal Government infinitely outweigh the debt incurred by the operations of the Board of Public Works. If Shepherd, however, had been able to foresee that Congress would one day renege on its obligations to the District and gradually reduce its contribution to the budget until today it amounts to less than 8%, it is doubtful whether he would have consented so willingly to the elimination of popular suffrage in the national capital."

(This amazing glimpse can be found at
https://www.jstor.org/stable/40067299)

The Organic Act of 1871

I hope you got as lost in that story as I did. I found that absolutely fascinating! I can picture the outfits, the horse-drawn carriages, and the hustle and bustle of the crowded streets as I read that captivating glance back into American history.

But let's talk about this Act of 1871 more in depth. Like many other writings, I find it to be of extreme importance to document anything I bring to you. Here is the Act of 1871 in all its glory. The Act will be in italics and my comments following any segments I want to comment on will not.

"CHAP. LXII – An Act to provide a Government for the District of Columbia."

Let's pause here. This is the beginning of the Act. The title. Those who are confused by the Act itself are often adding in text from the original common law that falls above this Act. On the next page, locate this chapter heading on the document midway down. This is where the Act begins.

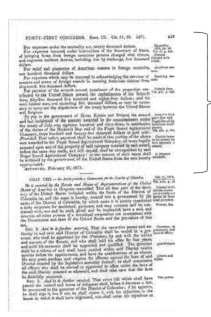

This is not part of the Act of 1871

Notice that the page starts with "For expenses under the neutrality act, twenty thousand dollars."

The way common law was organized at our founding is quite different than it is today. Back then they literally wrote everything down in chronological order. They also did not start a new page between issues they took up during the same session. Notice just above the start of the paragraph at the top of the page you see the title,

"FORTY-FIRST CONGRESS. Sess. III CH. 61, 62. 1871"

This first paragraph, followed by two stand-alone sentences and two more paragraphs is not part of the Organic Act of 1871. In order to see what this portion pertains to one must flip back a couple of pages to learn what this information is discussing. In doing so, we learn that this same Congress, on the same day they took up the matter of the Act of 1871 also enacted another act as you see at the top of page 417, a couple of pages prior to the chapter containing the Act of 1871. Let's take a look together. On the next page, you see the chapter and chapter title, introducing this legislation for an Act making Appropriations for the consular and diplomatic expenses for the government for the year ending June 30, 1872, and for other purposes.

(Hey, sleuth, feel free to use this blank space to jot down your thoughts and questions.)

CHAP. LXI. — *An Act making Appropriations for the consular and diplomatic Expenses*   Feb. 21, 1871.
of the Government for the Year ending June thirty, eighteen hundred and seventy-two, and
for other Purposes.

Be it enacted by the Senate and House of Representatives of the United
States of America in Congress assembled, That the following sums be, and   Consular and
the same are hereby, appropriated, out of any money in the treasury not   diplomatic ex-
otherwise appropriated, for the objects hereinafter expressed, for the fiscal   penses appropri-
year ending June thirty, eighteen hundred and seventy-two, namely : —   ation.

For salary of envoys extraordinary and ministers plenipotentiary to   Envoys and
Great Britain and France, at seventeen thousand five hundred dollars   ministers pleni-
each, thirty-five thousand dollars.   potentiary.

To Russia, Prussia, Spain, Austria, Brazil, Mexico, China, and Italy,
at twelve thousand dollars each, ninety-six thousand dollars.

To Chili, Peru, and Japan, ten thousand dollars each, thirty thousand
dollars.

For ministers resident at Portugal, Switzerland, Greece, Belgium,   Ministers resi-
Holland, Denmark, Sweden, Turkey, Ecuador, New Granada, Bolivia,   dent.
Venezuela, Guatemala, Nicaragua, Sandwich Islands, Costa Rica, Hon-
duras, and Salvador, at seven thousand five hundred dollars each, one
hundred and thirty-five thousand dollars.

For minister resident at the Argentine Republic, seven thousand five
hundred dollars.

For minister to Uruguay, accredited also to Paraguay, eleven thousand
two hundred and fifty dollars.

For salary of minister resident and consul-general at Hayti, seven   Hayti and Li-
thousand five hundred dollars.   beria.

For salary of minister resident and consul-general at Liberia, four
thousand dollars.

For salaries of secretaries of legation, as follows : —   Secretaries of
At London and Paris, two thousand six hundred and twenty-five dol-   legation and as-
lars each, five thousand two hundred and fifty dollars.   sistants.

At Saint Petersburg, Madrid, Berlin, Florence, Vienna, Rio de Janeiro,
and Mexico, one thousand eight hundred dollars each, twelve thousand
six hundred dollars.

For salaries of assistant secretaries of legation at London and Paris,
two thousand dollars each, four thousand dollars.

For salary of the secretary of legation, acting as interpreter to the   Interpreters.
legation to China, five thousand dollars.

For salary of the secretary of legation to Turkey, acting as interpreter,
three thousand dollars.

For salary of the interpreter to the legation to Japan, two thousand
five hundred dollars.

For contingent expenses of foreign intercourse proper and all contin-   Contingent ex-
gent expenses of all missions abroad, one hundred thousand dollars.   penses.

To enable Robert C. Schenck, minister to Great Britain, to employ a   Private aman-
private amanuensis, according to joint resolution approved January   uensis for Robert
eleven, eighteen hundred and seventy-one, two thousand five hundred   C. Schenck.
dollars.   Pub. Res. No. 6.
    Post, p. 590.

For salaries of consuls-general, consuls, vice-consuls, commercial   Consuls-gen-
agents, and thirteen consular clerks, including loss by exchange thereon,   eral, consuls, &c.
namely, three hundred and ninety-one thousand and two hundred dol-
lars :

I. CONSULATES GENERAL.   Consulates
    general.

Schedule B.   Schedule B.

Alexandría, Calcutta, Constantinople, Frankfort-on-the-Main, Havana,
Montreal, Shanghai, Beirut, Tampico, London, Paris.

Consulates.

Schedule B.

II. CONSULATES.

SCHEDULE B.

Aix-la-Chapelle, Acapulco, Algiers, Amoy, Amsterdam, Antwerp, Aspinwall, Bangkok, Basle, Belfast, Buenos Ayres, Bordeaux, Bremen, Brindisi, Boulogne, Barcelona, Cadiz, Callao, Canton, Chemnitz, Chin Kiang, Clifton, Coaticook, Cork, Demerara, Dundee, Elsinore, Fort Erie, Foo-Choo, Funchal, Geneva, Genoa, Gibraltar, Glasgow, Goderich, Halifax, Hamburg, Havre, Honolulu, Hong-Kong, Hankow, Hakodadi, Jerusalem, Kanagawa, Kingston, (Jamaica,) Kingston, (Canada,) La Rochelle, Laguayra, Leeds, Leghorn, Leipsic, Lisbon, Liverpool, Lyons, Malaga, Malta, Manchester, Matanzas, Marseilles, Mauritius, Melbourne, Messina, Munich, Mahe, Nagasaki, Naples, Nassau, (West Indies,) New Castle, Nice, Nantes, Odessa, Oporto, Osaca, Palermo, Panama, Pernambuco, Pictou, Port Mahon, Port Said, Prescott, Prince Edward Island, Quebec, Rio de Janeiro, Rotterdam, San Juan del Sur, San Juan, (Porto Rico,) Saint John's, (Canada East,) Santiago de Cuba, Port Sarnia, Rome, Singapore, Smyrna, Southampton, Saint Petersburg, Santa Cruz, (West Indies,) Saint Thomas, Spezzia, Stutgardt, Swatow, Saint Helena, Tangier, Toronto, Trieste, Trinidad de Cuba, Tripoli, Tunis, Tunstall, Turk's Island, Valparaiso, Vera Cruz, Vienna, Valencia, Windsor, Yeddo, Zurich, Birmingham, Barmen, and Winnepeg (Selkirk settlement, British North America.)

Commercial agencies.

Schedule B.

III. COMMERCIAL AGENCIES.

SCHEDULE B.

Madagascar, San Juan del Norte, San Domingo.

Consulates.

Schedule C.

IV. CONSULATES.

SCHEDULE C.

Aux Cayes, Bahia, Batavia, Bay of Islands, Cape Haytien, Candia, Cape Town, Carthagena, Ceylon, Cobija, Cyprus, Falkland Islands, Fayal, Guayaquil, Guaymas, Maranham, Matamoras, Mexico, Montevideo, Omoa, Payta, Para, Paso del Norte, Piraeus, Rio Grande, Saint Catharine, Saint John, (Newfoundland,) Santiago, (Cape Verde,) Stettin, Tabasco, Tahiti, Talcahuano, Tumbez, Venice, Zanzibar.

Commercial agencies.

V. COMMERCIAL AGENCIES.

Amoor River, Apia, Belize, Gaboon, Saint Paul de Loanda, Lanthala, Sabinilla.

Interpreters.

For interpreters to the consulates in China, Japan, Siam, and Turkey, including loss by exchange thereon, five thousand eight hundred dollars.

Marshals for consular courts.

For salaries of the marshals for the consular courts in Japan, including that at Nagasaki, and in China, Siam, and Turkey, including loss by exchange thereon, seven thousand seven hundred dollars.

Stationery, &c.

For stationery, book-cases, arms of the United States, seals, presses, and flags, and payment of rent, freight, postage, and miscellaneous expenses, including loss by exchange, sixty thousand dollars.

Consulates in Turkish dominions.

For expenses for interpreters, guards, and other matters, at the consulates at Constantinople, Smyrna, Candia, Alexandria, Jerusalem, and Beirut, in the Turkish dominions, three thousand dollars.

Prisons for American convicts.

For rent of prisons for American convicts in Japan, China, Siam, and Turkey, and for wages of the keepers of the same, including loss by exchange, twenty-one thousand seven hundred and fifty dollars.

Page 418 clearly has not completed the conversation concerning this appropriations act. It continues onto page 419, where we bump into the Organic Act of 1871 mid-way down. Refer back to page 45 for page 419.

At the bottom of these few paragraphs that fill the top portion of page 419 we see the words,

"APPROVED, February 21, 1871."

The act that started on page 417 has been approved by Congress.

The next line and next chapter heading, is Congress taking up the next order of business that day in the chamber. They closed the books on the first order of business and now have moved on to topic number two.

Because the Act sits underneath a conversation about finances it has been mistaken for being part of the information above it. But because common law was formerly logged in chronological order, this was just the flow of the order of business that particular day.

Today our common law has been completely revamped into a much better system that is not so cumbersome. Can you imagine trying to find a law just by trying to recall or having to log which day of which year something was written? What a terribly inefficient and unsustainable way to run a country!

In the early days of the United States, laws were written down as they were created, leading to a system where legal rules were scattered and often difficult to find. This system followed a common law tradition, where decisions were based on precedent rather than a comprehensive legal code.

Code simply means a well-structured library where laws are categorized by their content or subject matter. This allows for easier access, understanding, and reference to the various laws that govern a society. Instead of a scattered and ad-hoc approach, a comprehensive legal code provides a unified and clear structure for the legal system.

As society and the legal system evolved, there was a growing recognition of the need for a more organized and accessible legal system. Enter the process of codification. Imagine it as a makeover for the legal structure. Codification involves systematically arranging and organizing laws into a structured legal code.

The U.S. Code is like a well-organized library for federal laws. It categorizes and compiles laws by subject matter, making them easier to find and understand.

Hopefully, that clears up some cobwebs from conversations you may have been privy to that suggested code was some sort of bad word in correlation with our common laws. We basically gave our laws a Dewey decimal system of sorts.

A bit of a bunny trail here. If you have not read my first publication, *Patriot Psyop: The Battle For Your Mind"* this discussion is also pertinent when discussing 50 USC 1550 which has been mistaken for part of the War Powers Resolution Act because of where it is organized into code, but in fact, it is not part of WPRA. It is from NDAA but was organized into code beneath the WPRA by Congress and its placement in code was signed off by President Joe Biden.

So, as you read through the old document where the Organic Act of 1871 was written down in the old chronological system, you see firsthand how Congress operated back then. It's a fascinating glimpse into yesteryear. But it also clears up any confusion that has been mixed in with the understanding of the Act as it pertains to money changing hands.

Moving along to the Act itself, the first paragraph sets up the content for the entire act.

"Be it enacted by the Senate and House of Representatives of the United States of America in Congress assembled. That all that part of the territory of the United States included within the limits of the District of Columbia be, and the same is hereby, created into a government by the name of District of Columbia, by which name it is hereby constituted **a body corporate for municipal purposes...***"*

I am not through the chapter yet, but let me pause here. This already shows the complete intent of the act. It is setting up municipal government for the locals. Now you may be asking "why" when that was already accomplished in both 1801 and then revised in 1807? Hold tight. We will get to that.

Let's continue:

"...and may contract and be contracted with, sue and be sued, plead and be impleaded, have a seal, and exercise all other powers of a **municipal corporation not inconsistent with the Constitution and laws of the United States** *and the provisions of this act."*

There is likely some confusing language there. We will work through all of it. But notice that last part. "not inconsistent with the Constitution and laws of the United States..."

If you hear nothing else, know that this act comes up underneath the Constitution, the supreme law of the land.

I am not going to place the whole act here in the body of the book; however, the whole document is in the appendix for you to read. Please do. It is an impressive document.

As you continue to read, you see how it is explicitly stated that all must come under the law.

Nothing about this act is tied to England or the Vatican in any way shape or form.

As you refer back to the chapter entitled "Incorporation" on page 9 you now understand what it means to create a municipal corporation. I encourage you to look up the corporation or lack thereof in your area. This will concrete your understanding of municipal corporations.

Back to 1801 and the very first municipal corporation that was formed in the District of Columbia for the locals there, there were problems with that municipality that we mentioned back in the chapter titled "DC Inc.". Please keep in mind that all of this was a new experiment. These brilliant men were forming a whole new nation. They didn't nail everything perfectly the first time. They had to redo things and often multiple times. Even our beloved U.S. Constitution was the second attempt. The Revised Act of 1807 was more helpful to the citizens of the area as we discussed. The Act of 1871 was another improvement for the locals as well. However, there were new issues with new growing pains and new hurdles to jump. 1871 was replaced seven short years later with the District of Columbia Organic Act of 1878. Why?

There was indeed, financial mismanagement. The concern over financial management and corruption in the District stemmed from issues that arose after the implementation of the Act of 1871. Under this new system, the District was governed by a governor appointed by the President of the United States and a board of commissioners. This centralized governance structure led to several problems:

1. Lack of Accountability: The appointed officials were not directly accountable to the residents of the District, leading to concerns about transparency and oversight.

2. Mismanagement of Funds: There were allegations of mismanagement and misuse of public funds by the appointed officials, including reports of embezzlement and wasteful spending.

3. Conflict of Interest: The board of commissioners had significant authority over contracts and expenditures in the District, leading to potential conflicts of interest and favoritism in awarding contracts.

4. Limited Representation: residents of the District had limited or no representation in the government that governed them, which raised concerns about democratic principles and the consent of the governed.

These issues, along with the broader desire for local control and representation, contributed to the push to repeal the Act of 1871 and restore a form of government that provided for more democratic governance and accountability in the District of Columbia.

It is of note that none of these issues included any foreign countries

The District of Columbia Organic Act of 1878 reinstated a form of government for the District of Columbia similar to the one before the Act of 1871, with the District divided into two counties, Washington County and the County of Georgetown, each with its own government. This change was primarily motivated by concerns about the concentration of power in the hands of a single appointed governor and board of commissioners, which led to these list of issues.

In 1895, once again and for the final time, the Georgetown section of Washington County was consolidated with the City of Washington, effectively merging the two entities into a single municipal government. This consolidation was part of a series of changes that gradually unified the governance of the District of Columbia into a single, unified municipal government.

Over the years, the governance structure of the District has continued to evolve. Various laws, regulations, and amendments have been enacted that have shaped the governance of the District, including the Home Rule Act of 1973. This act granted the District limited self-government, with an elected mayor and council, significantly changing the governance structure and giving residents more control over local affairs.

The Mind Game

So why are people misconstruing the meaning of the Act of 1871 and turning it into something it clearly is not? THAT is a great question!

I will now tell you the disinformation as if it's real and then we will take it all apart piece by piece. We'll take it from the perspective of the storytellers.

The story goes like this:

Imagine a hidden truth, buried beneath layers of deception and manipulation, that reveals a shocking reality about the United States. The Act of 1871 is not just a simple piece of legislation—it is the key that unlocks the secret to understanding who truly controls America.

the Act of 1871 was a carefully orchestrated plan by powerful forces to transform the United States into a corporation. This corporation, known as the "United States of America, Inc.," is not the government we think it is. Instead, it is a corporate entity owned and controlled by foreign interests, specifically the City of London and the Vatican.

This nefarious plan began long before the Civil War, as these foreign powers sought to gain control over the burgeoning American nation. By the time of the Civil War, the United States was deeply in debt, and this debt became the leverage that allowed these foreign entities to exert their control.

Through the Act of 1871, the federal government was reorganized as a corporation owned by London and the Vatican since the US was deeply in debt to them because of the Civil War. Ever since the act of 1871, citizens have been considered employees or assets of this corporation. Your social security number is really a corporate EIN upon which they trade. The District of Columbia, which was already a municipal corporation, became the headquarters of this new corporate government. The use of legal language and terminology, such as the capitalization of certain words, was used to deceive the American people into believing that they were still living under a constitutional government, when in fact they were now subject to corporate rule. There are two classes of citizens: those who are part of the "United States of America, Inc." and those who are not.

Furthermore, why would a new municipal corporation need to take place in 1871 when there was already one created in 1801? They tricked you.

To further solidify this nefarious hidden usurpation of the Constitution, consider how there are matching obelisks in London, the Vatican, and the District of Columbia! It is evidence hidden in plain sight that a dirty deal was made to sell you to the control of the crown. These mark the symbol of their secret alliance. Symbolism will be their downfall.

Here is the necessary documentation to prove that The United States is owned by the crown and that we are The United States, Inc.

As you can see, this is a stock certificate showing that the United States is owned by the crown.

Reality Check

let's take a look at what these pictures really are. Examining the first picture, the United States Crown Corporation Common Stock, what else do you see when examining this document? Keep in mind that this certificate has been named as the proof by "Dr." Jan Halper Hayes, born and raised, working and living in London, England, that the United States was turned into a corporation through the Act of 1871.

In the center of the certificate, what do you see there? This symbol. It is a crown-shaped bottle cap company.

What else do you notice on the certificate? At the bottom, there is a circular seal that tells us the year this company became a corporation. 1960. This is verified when going to "Open Corporates" where corporations are transparently identified, along with their status over time. Upon further investigation there, the exact date of incorporation was February 2, 1960.

Let's talk about the stock certificate and the founder for a sec. This is what a seller of the certificates has to say about this bottle cap company and its founder.

"Stock printed by Security-Columbian Banknote Company. Available in Blue, Brown or Burgundy. Please specify color. Maybe related to Crown Holdings, Inc., formerly Crown Cork & Seal Company, which is an American company that makes metal beverage and food cans, metal aerosol containers, metal closures and specialty packing. Founded in 1892, it is headquartered in Yardley, Pennsylvania. As of their annual report for 2020, Crown employs 33,264 people at 192 plants in 39 countries. It claims to manufacture one out of every five beverage cans used in the world, and one out of every three food cans used in North America and Europe. The company is ranked No. 286 in the Fortune 500 list for 2022 and is number one in the packaging and container industry for the same list. William Painter, an Irish-born American, invented the crown cap for bottled carbonated beverages in 1891 and obtained patents 468,226 and 468,258 for it on February 2, 1892. He founded his own manufacturing business, the Crown Cork and Seal Company, in Baltimore and set out on a campaign to convince bottlers that his cap was the right one to use on their products. By 1898, he had created a foot-powered crowner device to sell to bottlers and retailers so that they could seal the bottles with his caps quickly and easily. This helped gain

acceptance of his bottle caps. By 1906, Crown had opened manufacturing plants in Brazil, France, Germany, Japan, and the United Kingdom. Read more at https://en.wikipedia.org/wiki/Crown_Holdings Item ordered may not be exact piece shown. All original and authentic" (2024onlineshop.ru, n.d.).

Notice that this particular stock certificate which was obviously pulled from Ebay and another collectibles shop by those pushing this narrative is dated November 1, 1971. That was the date of sale of this particular stock.

Looking at our supposed timeline for the erroneous and false capture of Constitutional America by "the crown" and the Vatican, turning the US into a corporation, that was said to take place in 1871. The bank that supplied this stock certificate was not even founded until the year 1879, and this private bottle cap company was not incorporated until the year 1960.

Clearly, anyone pushing this private company's stock certificate as proof of the United States Constitution being supplanted by a backroom deal between American individuals, London, and the Vatican, has nothing but manipulation in mind. The question I will continually want you to ask is "Why?"

(Off-topic and a curiosity of mine, because I am sometimes Curious George, I wonder if there are still any of these relics for sale.)

Bankrupted Corporation Documents?

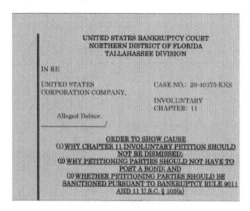

"United States Bankruptcy Court Northern District of Florida Tallahassee Division" and "United States Corporation Company"

Let me explain what the United States Corporation Company is before we go any further.

Every state has one. Here is a clip taken from the internet showing the first few. I was not able to grab the whole list in one picture.

Process Agents for: UNITED STATES CORPORATION COMPANY

State	Representative Name/ Company Name	Address
AK	UNITED STATES CORPORATION COMPANY	6505 OLD DAIRY RD STE 205 JUNEAU AK 99801
AL	UNITED STATES CORPORATION COMPANY	641 SOUTH LAWRENCE STREET MONTGOMERY AL 36104
AR	UNITED STATES CORPORATION COMPANY	350 BPR BLDG STE900500 S SPRING ST LITTLE ROCK AR 72201
AZ	UNITED STATES CORPORATION COMPANY	9622-N 23RD AVENUE SUITE 100 PHOENIX AZ 85021
CA	UNITED STATES CORPORATION COMPANY	2710 GATEWAY OAKS DRIVE, SUITE 150N SACRAMENTO CA 95833
CO	UNITED STATES CORPORATION COMPANY	1900 W LITTLETON BOULEVARD LITTLETON CO, 80120
CT	UNITED STATES CORPORATION COMPANY	GOODWIN SQ 225 ASYLUM ST 20TH FLOOR HARTFORD CT, 06103
DC	UNITED STATES CORPORATION COMPANY	1090 VERMONT AVE, N.W. WASHINGTON DC, 20005
DE	UNITED STATES CORPORATION COMPANY	251 LITTLE FALLS DRIVE WILMINGTON DE, 19808-1674
FL	UNITED STATES CORPORATION COMPANY	1201 HAYS STREET, STE 105 TALLAHASSEE, FL, 32301
GA	UNITED STATES CORPORATION COMPANY	2 SUN COURT SUITE 400 PEACHTREE CORNERS GA, 30092
HI	UNITED STATES CORPORATION SYSTEM, INC	1003 BISHOP ST, STE, 1600 PAUAHI HONOLULU HI, 96813
IA	UNITED STATES CORPORATION COMPANY	505 5TH AVENUE, SUITE 729 DES MOINES IA, 50309
ID	UNITED STATES CORPORATION COMPANY	1300 12TH AVENUE ROAD NAMPA, ID, 83686

Here is the website where you can find where your state's office is located.

https://li-public.fmcsa.dot.gov/LIVIEW/pkg_html.prc_proc_servers?cov_id=22&

Seems strange, doesn't it? Why does every state have one of these offices? What is its purpose and function?

Corporations use a company like the United States Corporation Company (USCC) for administrative support, including incorporation and registered agent services.

What is a registered agent service? Great question. An RA service is a designated individual or entity appointed by a corporation or LLC to receive legal documents, official notices, and other important correspondence on behalf of the business.

The registered agent's primary role is to ensure that the business remains compliant with state regulations by promptly receiving and forwarding legal documents, such as services of process (lawsuits), tax notices, and other official communications from government agencies.

Having a registered agent is a legal requirement for all corporations and LLCs. The registered agent's name and address must be provided in the business's formation documents and maintained throughout its existence.

RA services are often provided by specialized companies that offer this service for a fee. These companies help corporations and LLCs remain in good standing.

This USCC agency was established in 1925. It was a conglomerate formed by several large corporations, including General Motors, Standard Oil, and U.S. Steel, with the aim of providing these registered agent services to its member companies operating in multiple states.

The USCC essentially acted as a central administrative hub for its member corporations, streamlining processes like incorporation, filing annual reports, and managing legal matters across different states. By centralizing these services, member corporations could benefit from economies of scale and greater efficiency in their administrative operations. This is not a government entity. It is a private corporation formed by its member companies.

Not all corporations use the USCC or similar entities for incorporation and registered agent services. While the services provided by entities like the USCC are indeed essential for corporations to operate lawfully, corporations have flexibility in choosing who provides these services.

You can see here examples of companies who at some point chose to use USCC as their officer/Registered Agent.

Next List		United States Corporation C Search

Officer/Registered Agent Name List

Officer/RA Name	Entity Name	Entity Number
UNITED STATES CORPORATION COMPANY	LEVY'S	006541
UNITED STATES CORPORATION COMPANY	SUPERIOR OIL COMPANY	123494
UNITED STATES CORPORATION COMPANY	MIFLORA HOLDING CO INC	130597
UNITED STATES CORPORATION COMPANY	R C MOTOR LINES INC	132730
UNITED STATES CORPORATION COMPANY	DIXIE AUTO TRANSPORT COMPANY	137818
UNITED STATES CORPORATION COMPANY	NATIONAL BEVERAGES, INC.	138432
UNITED STATES CORPORATION COMPANY	CHEMCENTRAL CORPORATION	147636

There are many registered agent companies and legal service providers available that offer similar services to those provided by the USCC. Corporations may choose to use these alternative providers based on factors such as cost, reputation, geographic coverage, and specific service offerings.

So, while some corporations may have their officer or registered agent name listed as the United States Corporation Company, others may use different registered agent companies or handle these functions internally. It ultimately depends on the preferences and needs of each corporation.

Here are some choices:

1. Corporation Service Company

2. National Registered Agents, Inc. (NRAI)

3. Registered Agent Solutions, Inc. (RASi)

4. CT Corporation System (CT Corp)

5. InCorp Services, Inc.

6. Northwest Registered Agent, LLC

7. LegalZoom Registered Agent Services

8. Harvard Business Services, Inc.

9. Rocket Lawyer Registered Agent Services

10. BizFilings Registered Agent Services

These are just a few examples, and there are many other registered agent companies and service providers available.

Corporate Transparency

Did you know that it is the law that each state must make its corporations publicly transparent? Secretaries of States hire companies like Dun & Bradstreet, Sunbiz or Open Corporates which are companies that meet this need for your regulatory compliance. That's not to say they don't also offer other services. It is not required by law that the Secretary of State's office must create the system in-office to provide that transparency. They can outsource that task and most states, if not all, have done that with either Dun & Bradstreet, Sunbiz, or another organization called "Open Corporates."

Any changes made to your corporation status run through your your Secretary of State office who has likely partnered with one of these database transparency companies that specializes in this type of data housing to keep the public apprised of the status of your corporation. It might be a fun pursuit to find out from your Secretary of State office which of these or other companies they utilize to comply with transparency laws.

Sunbiz is the online filing system and database maintained by the Florida Department of State Division of Corporations. It allows individuals and businesses to search for and access information on corporations, limited liability companies, partnerships, and other business entities registered in the state of Florida. Sunbiz provides services related to business registration, filing annual reports, and accessing corporate records but does not function as a registered agent service.

Dun & Bradstreet offers a wide range of business information and commercial data analytics services, including credit reports, risk management solutions, marketing insights, and business intelligence. They collect data from various sources, including public records, financial filings, and proprietary databases, to provide comprehensive business information to their clients.

Open Corporates" happens to be based in Wales. However, their only task is to provide transparency. They do not own any part of these corporations. They only broadcast the status of the corporation itself. Your Secretary of State has contracted with that company, or another, to be the entity that helps them stay compliant with the law. The corporation is still lawfully abiding under the corporation laws of the individual state it was created in and is therefore subject not only to the constitution of that state but also the constitution of the United States.

"Open Corporates" is a platform that aggregates corporate data from around the world and makes it accessible for search and analysis. It collects information from public sources, such as government registries and official records, and provides a searchable database of corporate entities, including their corporate structure, officers, and filing history. Open Corporates aims to promote transparency and access to corporate information, which is perfect for meeting the legal requirements in your state.

While Dun & Bradstreet and Open Corporates provide access to business information, Dun & Bradstreet focuses more on commercial data analytics and risk management solutions for business, while Open Corporates focuses on providing a platform for accessing and analyzing corporate data for research and transparency purposes.

In the appendix I have put the entire six pages of the Articles of Incorporation of the United States Corporation Company, created in July of 1925.

Whitehouse D&B

Some folks are confused as to why the White House has Dunn and Bradstreet listings. They say it points to the White House, and thus the federal government being a corporation instead of what it actually is.

Let me explain:

The listing for the White House includes basic business information for several possible reasons:

1. While the White House is not a business entity, it is a government entity that engages in various administrative and operational activities. Government entities, including federal agencies, and departments, and offices, may be listed in commercial databases like D&B for informational purposes.

2. The White House may interact with external vendors, contractors, or service providers for various purposes, such as procurement, event planning, or facility management. Having a listing in the D&B business directory may help facilitate communication and business relationships with external entities.

3. Listing government entities in commercial databases like D&B can enhance transparency and accessibility of information about government operations. It allows businesses, researchers, and the public, to access basic information about government entities and their activities.

The White House is not a corporation. It is the official residence and workplace of the President and his staff, and it serves as the executive branch of the federal government. While the White House may engage in certain administrative operational activities, it is a government entity, not a commercial business.

Entities listed on the D&B business directory can include a wide range of organizations, including corporations, government agencies, non-profit organizations, sole proprietorships, and partnerships. The listing on D&B is primarily for informational and identification purposes and does not indicate corporate status.

Revealing the Full Document

Now that we have laid the groundwork for what the United States Corporation Company is and is not, let's get back to that clip again that was circulated on social media as supposed proof of Trump bankrupting the United States Corporation and take a closer look at this document. I find it incredibly revealing that individuals set on subverting your mind pushed this small portion of this document. It really doesn't take much to go look this document up since it gives the address of which case it is.

All that has to be done is a Google search of case number 20-40375-KKS. And guess what happens when you do? You quickly notice that the actual case is worded differently than the small clip that has been floating around social media. It has been altered. Let's have a closer look.

UNITED STATES BANKRUPTCY COURT
NORTHERN DISTRICT OF FLORIDA
TALLAHASSEE DIVISION

IN RE:

UNITED STATES   CASE NO.: 20-40375-KKS
CORPORATION COMPANY,
                                                 INVOLUNTARY
                                                 CHAPTER: 11
    Alleged Debtor.
_____/

ORDER ENJOINING PETITIONING PARTY, SYTERIA HEPHZIBAH, A/K/A HIGHLY FAVORED SHEKINAH EL, PURSUANT TO *ORDER FOR PETITIONING PARTY, SYTERIA HEPHZIBAH, TO SHOW CAUSE WHY SHE SHOULD NOT BE DECLARED A VEXATIOUS LITIGANT* (DOC. 38)

THIS MATTER came before the Court for hearing on December 17, 2020, on the *Order for Petitioning Party, Syteria Hephzibah, to Show Cause Why She Should Not Be Declared a Vexatious Litigant* ("Order to Show Cause," Doc. 38). Petitioning Party, Syteria Hephzibah, a/k/a Highly Favored Shekinah-El ("Hephzibah a/k/a Shekinah-El"), appeared.[1]

Having considered the record and testimony at the hearing, the Court finds that Hephzibah a/k/a Shekinah-El failed to show any cause

_____

[1] Syteria Hephzibah designates herself as "Highly Favored Shekinah El, dba Moorish Science Temple of America, dba Court of Equity and Truth, Lawful Beneficiary Creditor, Heir of the Vast Estate . . . ." The hearing was conducted telephonically due to the continuing COVID-19 pandemic.

NJM

69

why this Court should not declare her a vexatious litigant.

BACKGROUND

Hephzibah a/k/a Shekinah-El has commenced two (2) bankruptcy cases and three (3) adversary proceedings in this Court, including the instant case. She has also filed numerous cases in state and other federal courts.[2] She has sued or attempted to sue federal, state, and local agencies, their employees, attorneys, judges, and other private persons and entities.[3] This Court and others have determined that cases and claims filed by Hephzibah a/k/a Shekinah-El, other than the Chapter 7 bankruptcy petition filed in this Court in 2018,[4] were, among other things, frivolous, baseless, and vexatious.[5]

---

[2] A brief summary of Hephzibah's filing history in this Court and others can be found in the Order to Show Cause Doc. 38 and *Gullet-El v. Corrigan*, No. 3:17-cv-881-J-32JBT, 2017 WL 10861313 (M.D. Fla. Sept. 20, 2017).

[3] Docs. 1-7 & 1-8; Doc. 38, p. 5 n.14; *Gullet-El*, 2017 WL 10861313, at *1–4.

[4] *Chapter 7 Voluntary Petition, In re Hephzibah*, No. 18-40381-KKS (Bankr. N.D. Fla. July 18, 2018), Doc. 1.

[5] *Gullett-El*, 2017 WL 10861313, at *1–4 (dismissing complaint with prejudice as frivolous and vexatious and noting other courts that have determined cases filed by Hephzibah a/k/a Shekinah-El to be frivolous, baseless, and vexatious); Doc. 38, pp. 3–8 (citing this Court's previous warnings to Hephzibah a/k/a Shekinah-El from her Chapter 7 bankruptcy case and adversary proceedings); *Order Granting Alleged Debtor's Emergency Motion for Order Dismissing Involuntary Petition (Doc. 28)*, Doc. 45 (dismissing the Involuntary Petition with prejudice); *Order Enjoining Petitioning Parties Pursuant to Order to Show Cause (1) Why Chapter 11 Involuntary Petition Should Not Be Dismissed; (2) Why Petitioning Parties Should Not Have to Post a Bond; and (3) Whether Petitioning Parties Should be Sanctioned Pursuant to Bankruptcy Rule 9011 and 11 U.S.C. § 105 (Doc. 34)*, Doc. 49 (finding that the Involuntary Petition was meritless and was filed for an improper purpose); *see also Gullett v. Duff*, No. 19-2015, 2019 WL 3349962, *1 (D.D.C. July 24, 2019) ("Plaintiff [Gullett] and his mother [Hephzibah a/k/a Shekinah-El] are 'no strangers' to the United States District Court

2

In an effort to curtail her pattern of abuse, in 2017 the District
Court for the Middle District of Florida entered an injunction against
Hephzibah a/k/a Shekinah-El, enjoining her from filing suit in that court
and the Circuit Court for Duval County, Florida, without prior approval
from the District Court.[6] After that injunction issued, Hephzibah a/k/a
Shekinah-El came to this Court to continue her vexatious litigation.

The Order to Show Cause issued by this Court provides:

> Currently before the Court is Hephzibah's most recent filing—
> a Chapter 11 Involuntary Petition ("Involuntary Petition")
> against "United States Corporation Company" ("Alleged
> Debtor.") For the reasons that follow, and others that may be-
> come evident, the Court enters this Order to Show Cause to
> determine whether Hephzibah should be declared a vexatious
> litigant for (1) attempting to relitigate meritless and frivolous
> claims, (2) harassing Alleged Debtor, governmental agencies
> of the United States, and others, and (3) continuing to abuse
> the bankruptcy system.[7]

The Order to Show Cause also recited that two orders entered in the
Chapter 7 case filed by Hephzibah a/k/a Shekinah-El warned:

> [I]f [Hephzibah] continues filing papers with this Court in fur-
> ther attempts to obtain release from incarceration, she risks
> being declared a "vexatious litigant" and being assessed

---

for the Middle District of Florida, where 'each' has a history of filing 'patently frivolous and
vexatious' complaints.") (citing *Gullett-El*, 2017 WL 10861313, at *1).
[6] *Gullett-El*, 2017 WL 10861313, at *5. This injunction was also against Petitioning Party,
Taquan Rashe Gullett-El, a/k/a Maalik Rahshe El ("Gullet"). *Id.* at *1.
[7] Doc. 38, pp. 1–2 (footnote omitted).

3

sanctions under Fed. R. Bankr. P. 9011.[8]

> [Hephzibah] is again forewarned that if she continues filing papers in further attempt to obtain release from incarceration with this Court, she risks being declared a "vexatious litigant" and being assessed sanctions under Fed. R. Bankr. P. 9011.[9]

The Order to Show Cause reiterates that in the orders dismissing the three (3) adversary proceedings Hepzibah a/k/a Shekinah-El filed in 2018, this Court cautioned her that she could be deemed a vexatious litigant:

> [Hephzibah] is forewarned that if she continues filing adversary proceedings with this Court and then fails to properly prosecute them, she risks being declared a "vexatious litigant" and being assessed sanctions under Fed. R. Bankr. P. 9011.[10]

At the hearing on the Order to Show Cause, Hephzibah a/k/a Shekinah-El testified at length, describing in considerable detail her recollection of events, arrest(s), incarceration, and other incidents, some dating as far back as 2010. She described actions by various government authorities as "international war crimes" against her and her son, Gullett. Hephzibah a/k/a Shekinah-El further testified that she and her son

---

[8] *Id.* at p. 4 (quoting *Order Denying Debtor's Petition for Writ of Habeas Corpus and Other Relief (Doc. 45)* at 6, *In re Hephzibah*, No. 18-40381-KKS (Bankr. N.D. Fla. Feb. 12, 2019), Doc. 50).

[9] *Id.* at pp. 4–5 (quoting *Order Denying Motion for Contempt (Doc. 46)* at 2, *In re Hephzibah*, No. 18-40381-KKS (Bankr. N.D. Fla. Feb. 13, 2019), Doc. 51).

[10] *Id.* at pp. 5–6.

4

have unsuccessfully tried for years to obtain relief through the judicial system for these alleged crimes against them.

Apparently as a result of researching records of the Florida Department of State Division of Corporations, Hephzibah a/k/a Shekinah-El determined that Alleged Debtor, United States Corporation Company, a private entity based in Delaware, was the United States Government. According to her, filing the Involuntary Petition was another effort to "execute the process my son and I began to address international war crimes" and get relief from "heartache and pain" she and her son have allegedly been enduring at the hands of various federal and state officials for over six (6) years.

DISCUSSION

The Involuntary Petition has nothing to do with bankruptcy. None of the testimony at the Show Cause hearing reflects a scintilla of legal or factual support for filing an involuntary Chapter 11 petition against a private corporation unconnected with Hephzibah a/k/a Shekinah-El or the United States Government.

A bankruptcy court may use its inherent authority to sanction

5

parties for conduct that abuses the judicial process.[11] "This power is derived from the court's need to manage [its] own affairs so as to achieve
the orderly and expeditious disposition of cases."[12] "To impose sanctions
under the court's inherent power, the court must find bad faith."[13] Within
the Eleventh Circuit, a finding of bad faith may be warranted when a
party: (1) "knowingly or recklessly raises a frivolous argument, or argues
a meritorious claim for the purpose of harassing an opponent;"[14] (2) pur-
sues a claim without "reasonable inquiry into the underlying facts;"[15] or
(3) "continually advance[es] groundless and patently frivolous" claims.[16]

In addition to its inherent authority, a bankruptcy court "may
[also] invoke its statutory power of [§] 105(a) to redress Rule 9011 violations, bad faith, and unreasonable, vexatious litigation."[17] Under 11

---

[11] *Law v. Siegel,* 571 U.S. 415, 421 (2014) (citation omitted); *Glatter v. Mroz (In re Mroz),* 65 F.3d 1567, 1574–75 (11th Cir. 1995) (citing *Chambers v. NASCO, Inc.,* 501 U.S. 32, 43 (1991)); *In re Dekom,* No. 19-300082-KKS, 2020 WL 4004116, at *4 (Bankr. N.D. Fla. Apr. 6, 2020); *In re Pina,* 602 B.R. 72, 98 (Bankr. S.D. Fla. 2019); *In re Walker,* 414 B.R. 787, 791 (Bankr. M.D. Fla. 2009).
[12] *Ginsberg v. Evergreen Sec., Ltd. (In re Evergreen Sec., Ltd.),* 570 F.3d 1257, 1263 (11th Cir. 2009) (quoting *Bank of N.Y. v. Sunshine-Jr. Stores, Inc. (In re Sunshine Jr. Stores, Inc.),* 456 F.3d 1291,1304 (11th Cir. 2006)).
[13] *Id.* at 1273 (citing *In re Walker,* 532 F.3d 1304, 1309 (11th Cir. 2008)).
[14] *Id.* (quoting *Walker,* 532 F.3d at 1309).
[15] *Id.* at 1274 (quoting *Barnes v. Dalton,* 158 F.3d 1212, 1214 (11th Cir. 1998)).
[16] *Id.* (quoting *Glass v. Pfeffer,* 849 F.2d 1261, 1265 (10th Cir. 1988))
[17] *In re Zalloum,* No. 6-17-bk-02329-KSJ, 2019 WL 965098, at *9 (Bankr. M.D. Fla. Feb. 25, 2019) (citation omitted); *see also Jove Eng'g, Inc. v. IRS,* 92 F.3d 1539, 1543 (11th Cir. 1996) (distinguishing between a court's statutory power under § 105(a) and inherent power).

6

There are eight more pages. The remaining eight are in the appendix for you to peruse. I encourage you to read all of it to gain a full grasp of what this document truly is. Obviously, it is not what those intent on lying to you have told you it was.

Do you feel upset? Understandable. A lot of people have fallen for this psychological mind trap.

I just love my mind being messed with, don't you?

(Sarcasm is sometimes my love language.)

Inspecting "Moore" Evidence

In the third image, we encounter a document that appears to have been completely made up out of thin air. Extensive research into the White House archives has revealed no record of this document's existence. Had it originated from the White House, there would be a clear log documenting its creation.

May 4, 2020

RE: U.S. Federal Person "ROGER ALLEN MOORE/RAAJ AMEXEM MOOR RAFA EL"
Taxpayer Identification / Decedent's Social Security Number: 126-56-2363

Note: See United States Department of the Treasury/Internal Revenue Service Forms 2848 (Power of Attorney and Declaration of Representative) and 56 (Notice of Fiduciary Agent), sent December 1, 2019, via United States Postal Service Certified Mail Number 7016 0910 0002 3020 3644.

To whomever UNITED STATES Business Entity this may concern (who commercially-operates on United States Public Markets and excepts and/or exchanges in United States Currency while providing goods and/or services to U.S. Customers/Consumers in everyday commerce),

The above-mentioned U.S. Federal Public Person has a Pre-Paid Non-Obligatory Commercial Debt Obligation Arrangement with the UNITED STATES in relation to 12 U.S. Code § 95a – Regulation of Transactions in foreign exchange of gold and silver; property transfers; vested interests, enforcement and penalties (Part 2) and other Public Policy on U.S. Debt.

Your Business Entity is federally-bound to UNITED STATES and U.S. Public Debt Obligations, by way of your Internal Revenue Service Employer Identification Number (the I.R.S. being under the U.S. Department of the Treasury) and your Federal Reserve Business Bank Account.

Your Business is hereby ordered to itemize whatever and however many Commercial Products and/or Services in which the above U.S. Federal Public Person wishes to commercially-acquire, adjust the bottom line total cost amount to zero ($0.00), and release the items. Provide a receipt to the above U.S. Federal Person, by way of it's Duly Authorized Representative ("Raaj Rafa El – Sui Juris/De jure/In Proper Person") and retain the record of the transaction to settle with your Federal Tax Obligation(s) with Internal Revenue Service as the entire overall transaction is only a Commercial Accounting Matter of what the Bankrupt UNITED STATES owes it's True Creditors, which is the American People, in direct relation to the borrowed gold and National Banking Emergency Act of 1933. All Commercial Public Debt-Obligations, while transacting all business within UNITED STATES Commercial Markets, belong to the UNITED STATES, as the UNITED STATES is the True Obligor in each and every U.S. Commercial-Transaction.

Any Willful Dishonoring and/or Non-Settlement of UNITED STATES Commercial "Public-Debt" Obligational Matters, by any Duly-Bound Commercial Business Entity within the United States, will result in Federal Prosecution to the fullest extent possible.

Sincerely,

Donald J. Trump
President/Chief Executive Officer of the UNITED STATES

Upon closer examination, we encounter yet another individual claiming affiliation with the "Moorish" ideology, similar to what we observed with the previous document. A notable feature of this document is the inconsistent use of fonts. The heading at the top does not align with any known White House format, including internal communications.

Further scrutiny reveals a peculiar language pattern in the document. Such a messaging style is not consistent with any official White House or professionally printed document in circulation in Washington, D.C. Portions of the text are italicized or in bold, with numerous punctuation and grammatical errors throughout.

Additionally, certain words are capitalized, seemingly following the erroneous teachings of a group known as "Sovereign Citizens," who assert legal significance based on capitalization. However, there is no legal basis for such a claim. Furthermore, some words or letters are underlined without clear reason, and there are random hyphens in unusual places, all of which deviate from the standard format of formal legal documents, or even accepted English writing practice.

Notably, President Trump's signature appears unusually small, leading to doubts about its authenticity. Clearly, it has been copied and pasted here. President Trump has never signed any document referring to himself as "President/Chief Executive Officer of the UNITED STATES." This inconsistency is a forgery.

What is missing from this document that should be there?

1. Court Seal: Official court documents often bear the court's official seal, which is usually an embossed or raised emblem. Look for this seal as a key authenticity indicator. Is it there?

2. Court Header: Genuine court documents typically have a header at the top of the page that includes the

name of the court, case number, and the names of the parties involved. Is that there?

3. Court Signatures: Court documents include signatures of judges, clerks, or other court officials. These signatures should appear genuine, and you can cross-reference them with known court signatures if necessary. Is it there?

Even if this document were submitted to a court and accepted as evidence by a citizen, it would not validate its authenticity. It was purportedly submitted in Tallahassee, but it is important to note that submission does not equate to accuracy, validity, authenticity, or legal enforceability. Anyone can submit papers as evidence for their case. This document is undoubtedly a fabrication.

What is Moorish Society?

Looking further into this Moorish group, I did a deep dive to learn more about where this group came from. Here are clips from an impressive article by Omar Mouallem who went to these people and interviewed them to learn about this Moorish society. I've left out fluff, but you can read the full article through the URL I've provided in citations.

"I assumed my story would begin with the Nation's enigmatic founder, Wallace Fard Muhammad but in fact he had a predecessor. Noble Drew Ali, a man even more mystifying and arguably more consequential than Ali was the first American to tailor Islam to the conditions of Black people. And while his early 20th-century movement was always an outlier, he planted a seed that would see African American Islam grow in vigor and numbers, counting around half a million converts today across various branches. Few of those would be likely to recognize Ali's name or influence. But his obscure take on the Muslim faith

hasn't faded away — on the contrary, it's enjoying something of a revival.

Most scholars identify Ali as one Timothy Drew, an orphaned North Carolinian who discovered Islam somewhere in the U.S. northeast and founded the Moorish Science Temple of America sometime between 1913 and 1925. However, a recent book by historian Jacob S. Dorman says Ali was John Walter Brister, a Broadway child star and enigmatic circus performer who faked his death and reinvented himself as a Muslim prophet in Chicago. Ali, of course, told a different story. He taught followers he'd discovered a forgotten section of the Qur'an in North Africa, after a high priest of Egyptian magic had identified him as the reincarnation of Jesus and all other prophets. Ali's scripture, the Holy Koran of the Moorish Science Temple of America, often called the Circle 7, professed that there is "no negro, black, or colored race." African Americans were actually undeclared Moroccans, via ancient Muslim Moors.

Curiously, Ali's version of Moorish civilization bore little resemblance to that of any textbook. He told of a kingdom indigenous to northwestern and southwestern Africa and the Americas, and that still ruled over Morocco. As native Moors, he and millions of others were thus exempt from American segregation laws, so long as they had the right identity papers, which only Ali's temple could notarize (for a small fee).

Studied in tandem with the 1786 Moroccan-American Treaty of Friendship (the United States' oldest unbroken treaty with a foreign nation), Ali's teachings convinced thousands that they could break the shackles of white supremacy by taking his legal oath of Moorish American identity. It was both Black nationalism and denial; Ali's acolytes sincerely believed that they'd never be true citizens — and therefore free of abuse and mistreatment — until proclaiming Moorish nationality. While Moors have organized successful civic campaigns with real-life consequences (such as writing themselves into census surveys, which counted over 4,000 Moorish Americans between 2011 and 2015), their online presence looked more like performance art to me.

But Moorish beliefs are also predicated on pseudoscience. In Ali's doctrine, our nationalities and tribes fall into two categories, 'Asiatics' and 'Europeans.' The former, comprising Turks, Arabs, Asians, Africans, American Indigenous — what we would today describe as people of colour — are natural Muslims prepared for this earth by Allah, Jesus and Muhammad. The latter — what we would call white — invented Christianity in hopes of salvation. he began to evangelize his alternative history and notarize Moorish ID cards.

But Ali was extremely controversial within his community. According to reports at the time, Ali built temples in four states, gained 12,000 followers and amassed hoards of cash before his power began to unravel in 1929. One of Ali's closest aides went rogue and split off with several followers, until a team of men killed him in a suspected hit. Detained with others for the murder, Ali was eventually released on bond and died weeks later. the fallen leader had scammed a fortune from his followers and had two wives, one of whom was a minor.

These scandals hindered the efforts of acolytes to maintain the temple after his death. A further challenge was the number of new offshoots and impersonators tussling for his leadership, with more fatalities to follow. Membership fractured and went underground following this implosion, with some Moors gravitating to Wallace Fard Muhammad, who claimed to possess Ali's reincarnated spirit as he started the Nation of Islam.

Moorish Science seemed largely dormant when Jeff Fort reactivated it 45 years later, but his offshoot was also short-lived. In 1986, the FBI implicated Fort in a terrorism-for-hire sting involving Libya. Despite the brevity of his new movement, it's apparent that Fort — currently serving a 168-year sentence — preserved Moorish Science for future generations.

Believers fell into one of two groups called 'civic Moors' and 'temple Moors' by each other. The civic Moors nitpick about constitutions and declarations, and might view temple Moors as a bit too dogmatic. The temple Moors are into 'energies,' mysticism and Orientalist fashion. Their prejudices against civic Moors stem from those who take their Moorish citizenship to extremes.

A cursory search in Google News brings up regular headlines in which self-proclaimed Moors are charged for violating local traffic and property laws in eccentric ways: producing fake Moorish driver's licenses, disobeying eviction notices on convoluted grounds, or attempting to usurp properties using bizarre legalese. As a result, the Southern Poverty Law Center, a U.S. nonprofit that monitors homegrown extremism, designated Moorish sovereign citizens as an extremist group." (McIntyre, 2022)

You may be wondering how this information fits into the topic of the US as a corporation.

Honestly, it shouldn't and doesn't, other than the portion of this Moorish society that espouses the "Sovereign Citizen" ideology believe in this US corporation and these legal documents that include these Moorish society individuals have been propped up as the supposed "proof" that the US Constitution was in fact, usurped by the Organic Act of 1871 to create this fictitious corporation narrative.

Sovereign Citizens & State Nationals

R ecently, this Sovereign Citizen group has been working hard to rebrand itself as "State Nationals" because of the holes that have been exposed in the different twists and turns of this Sovereign Citizen narrative.

Here is how this goes. According to David Lester Strait, Anna Von Reitz, also known as Anna Marie Rietzinger, and others, the Organic Act somehow caused America to be under maritime law, as determined by the gold fringe on certain American flags. We'll cover that shortly. Because of that fact, according to Mr. Strait's cult teaching, each person is considered to be a "vessel," like a boat or some other watercraft, and calling someone a human being is tantamount to calling someone a monster.

People who were born in the United States who have a birth certificate and a social security number, according to them, are actually individual corporations the government is trading on but the secret trading floor's location is unknown, and this stock is not redeemable until the person is deceased. Words like air and heir, "doc"tor and "dock tender" mean the same thing. Your birth is also known as your "berth" and

83

the "dock tender" who gave berth to you got your parents to sign you over as a corporation instead of just being a human when they signed your birth certificate, as indicated by the bond paper your birth was recorded on. And of course, anything that is typed on bond paper means it is a "bond."

They sold you into slavery. There is a number imprinted on the back of that bond (birth certificate) which correlates with your ownership by the corporation. Your social security number is your corporate EIN. The way they justify that you are under maritime law is because you were birthed through your mother's watery canal. And again, the gold fringe flags flown by Trump point to this as proof.

Taking it a step further, these cult leaders assert that your driver's license is a tool of control. They overlook the fact that these licenses were established through state-by-state voting, primarily for safety and anti-theft purposes. Such narratives often trace back to the contentious Act of 1871, which these critics claim transformed the United States into a malevolent corporation.

According to proponents of the Sovereign Citizen and State National movements, true liberation requires shedding American citizenship and abandoning the identifiers that bind individuals to a perceived system of enslavement. The transition to State National status reflects a strategic shift, aimed at erasing the concept of "citizen" altogether. The grooming process is subtle yet methodical: first, individuals are encouraged to embrace sovereignty, and then they are persuaded to relinquish their citizenship entirely. This approach mirrors classic grooming techniques, where information is revealed incrementally to avoid arousing suspicion.

Advocates of this movement frame the transition as a mere change in status, from U.S. citizen to state national. In reality, however, this transition is not recognized by law. By promoting emotional appeals and misleading narratives, these groups attempt to persuade individuals to renounce their U.S. citizenship, despite the legal impossibility of becoming a "national" of a single state.

So, let's take apart each of these sand dunes this faulty structure is propped up on, starting with the gold-fringed flags. I would start with the Act itself, but the rest of the book has already completely covered that and has proven the narrative of a masterminded US corporation to be false.

Gold-Fringed Flags

There is an aspect of this narrative that stems from the fact that gold fringe is often seen around flags during Trump's administration.

What is maritime law? Maritime law, also known as admiralty law, is a distinct body of law that governs activities and issues that occur on navigable waters or involve maritime commerce. It covers a wide range of matters, including shipping, navigation, salvage, and maritime pollution. The application of maritime law is not indicated by the presence of a flag or any specific design element on a flag. Instead, it is determined by the nature of the activity or legal issue in question and the jurisdiction in which it occurs.

Maritime law can also apply to various issues involving navigable waters, including personal lakes or ponds if they are connected to navigable waters. It can also apply to structures on water, such as docks or piers, and issues related to boats and other vessels. The application of maritime law in these situations depends on various factors, including the specific circumstances and the jurisdiction in which the issue arises. Maritime law can also apply to matters such as maritime accidents, injuries that occur on ships or other vessels, maritime contracts, maritime liens, and issues related to cargo or goods transported by sea. It can also cover aspects of international trade, marine pollution, salvage operations, and more. But there is nothing about fringe on a flag that denotes maritime law. It simply does not. In truth, fringe on a flag is meaningless.

There is no hidden message conveyed by the presence of fringe on a flag that places individuals, entire countries, or any entity under admiralty law. Unless a situation involves bodies of water on one's property or falls into specific maritime law categories, admiralty law is not applicable.

Some individuals take offense at the addition of fringe to the flag, considering it a defacement. However, the tradition of adorning the flag with gold fringe dates back to 1835 and has been a part of formal dress for ceremonial purposes throughout American history. Claims that the presence of gold fringe on flags behind President Trump indicated his status as a wartime president are unfounded, as numerous presidents have appeared with gold-fringed flags in the background, indicating no special significance. This practice is well-documented in historical records and has been a common practice over the years.

What Does the Flag Code Say? The U.S. flag code does not explicitly mention the gold fringe flag, its uses, or any bans and permissions either. Fringe Flag Origins Looking at US history, the fringe was first seen on the American flag in 1835. Yet, it was not an official action, so in 1835 the fringes were officially added to the US flag for all Army regiments.

On the other hand, it is not illegal to fly a flag with fringes in the USA even when you don't belong to the army. More importantly, the fringe is just an honorable enrichment and does not confer admiralty or maritime jurisdiction.

Official Records and Statements: The first official record was in 1835, and from 1925, we have an opinion by the attorney general that the usage of the gold fringe is customary and not restricted to the Federal Government. A gold fringe American flag can be displayed by military, civic, and civilian organizations, as well as private individuals. Generally, there isn't a custom of using a fringed national flag as an internment flag, i.e., in prisons and similar institutions, nor are they normally seen on stationary flagpoles.

Why does the American flag have a gold fringe? To sum up, the gold fringe on the American flag is an honorable enrichment and it is in line with the military tradition. The fringes are purely decorative, but when you read between the lines, you will normally avoid flying such a flag in front of your home or business. The yellow fringe is more commonly seen on the indoor American flags, typically used as ceremonial flags for Veterans Day affairs or Memorial Day celebrations, typically carried by the American legion groups. Some flag sets come standard with gold fringe, and on others, it is an option to be added at no additional cost." (Carrot-Top Industries, N/A)

Washington D.C. Flag

Sovereign Citizens and State Nationals have distorted the meaning of a flag that features three red stars and two horizontal red stripes, which represents the municipality of Washington City in the District of Columbia. Although not a state, Washington City's flag serves as a symbol for its residents.

Designed after George Washington's family crest, this flag holds no sensational significance beyond what mainstream media sensationalism may imply. It is a common tactic to create drama and perpetuate conspiracies.

Bond Paper

Bond paper is used for many things; Stationary, photography, painting, drawings, blueprints, maps, and more. Architects use bond paper because it works in inkjets and pen plotter printers (Plotter Paper Guys).

The claim that your birth certificate, printed on bond paper somehow makes it a savings bond is silly. But it has caused so much confusion that people have bombarded the government seeking their payout for the bond that their birth certificate created. Here is the reply by the federal government.

"Several internet blogs and videos make false claims that a United States birth certificate is a negotiable instrument (a document that promises payment) that can be used to:

- *Make purchases that will be charged to a "Exemption Account" (perhaps identified by your social security number or EIN), or*
- *Request savings bonds held by the government in your name and owed to you.*

The truth is, birth certificates cannot be used for purchases, nor can they be used to request savings bonds purportedly held by the government. Also, the "Exemption Account" is a false term; these accounts are fictitious and do not exist in the Treasury system.

The Story

This story is a variation of the older Bogus Sight Drafts/Bills of Exchange Drawn on the Treasury scam.

The common tale offered in this scam states: When the United States went off the gold standard in 1933, the federal government somehow went bankrupt. With the help of the Federal Reserve Bank, the government became a corporation (sometimes called "Government Franchise") and converted the bodies of its citizens into capital value, supposedly by trading the birth certificates of U.S. citizens on the open market and making each citizen a corporate asset (sometimes referred to as a "Strawman") whose value is controlled by the government.

Scams vary in methods for citizens to gain control of their alleged assets, such as:

- *filing a UCC-1 Financial Statement,*
- *activating a TreasuryDirect Account (TDA), or*

- *creating bonds by using the Savings Bond Calculator.*

These blogs and videos promise that your birth certificate bond will be able to wipe out all your debt or help you collect monies/securities. Some internet sites even offer to sell videos, webinars, and coaching on how to do this. No one has profited from the Treasury Department by using these tactics. But the scammers intend to profit from this story by selling their bogus wares.

The Reality

There is no monetary value to a birth certificate or a social security number/EIN, and TreasuryDirect accounts must be funded by the owner (through payroll deductions or from purchasing directly from the owner's personal bank account) to have any value.

The Savings Bond Calculator is merely a tool to calculate the value of a bond based on an issue date and denomination entered. This information could be the issue date and denomination from a real bond, or it could just be a random choice of a date and denomination. The calculator only checks that the issue date and denomination entered are a valid combination - it will not verify whether a bond exists. The calculator will not verify the validity of a serial number or confirm bond ownership.

Please be advised that trying to defraud the government by claiming rights to bogus securities is a violation of federal law, and the Justice Department can and has prosecuted these crimes. Federal criminal convictions have occurred in several cases. The scam artists who post blogs and videos are trying to defraud you into buying their fake product. Do not fall victim to their schemes" (U.S. Department of the Treasury).

Importance of Research & Critical Thinking

Did you see that? This is a federal crime. Wow! So why would narrative leaders steer you to do this? Does this message target Democrats? Who is the main group of people heeding the whole idea of the United States Corporation psyop? It's clearly not geared toward the left-leaning demographic.

There is safety in scrutinizing all sides of information and becoming informed on both the proponents and the opponents of "theories" before choosing where to align your personal beliefs. Sometimes you may be unknowingly aligning with unlawful behavior. Spending a little bit of time researching all information, even when it appears to be coming from thought leaders who purport to have your best interest at heart, is wise. It is just as easy for a con artist to convince you of something as it is for someone who has only altruistic intentions.

Con artists study and learn the art of how to convince folks who enjoy even the highest emotional and mental acumen. If you suspect you might have been taken in by deception, do not think for a moment that this says something negative about you. No one is completely impervious to every deception that comes along. These folks are very skilled, and good at what they do, and they work hard to twist even the most fortified mind. It is sport for them. And many times it pays handsomely.

There are ways to minimize your exposure to manipulative narratives, and the most important one of all is slowing down, taking your time, and doing the important work of investigating all sides, no matter if those sides agree with your sensibilities, your political preference, your religion or your family's long-held beliefs. You will not regret grabbing all the information you can, and then synthesizing that down to make a truly educated decision.

If more people had searched and found the information here that to claim "rights to bogus securities is a violation of federal law, and the Justice Department can and has prosecuted these crimes," folks would have saved themselves time, money, and criminal records.

What has spun up out of this crazy notion of your birth certificate being a bond is quite nefarious when you follow it through to the end of its different machinations. One such trail leads to the suspicion of human trafficking.

How? Let's go there. Follow along with me on my train of thought here, and discover one of the possible scenarios this path leads to.

Trafficking

Current day, we are faced with the diabolical realization of the magnitude of the human trafficking pandemic that spans the globe. Personally, I cannot and will never be able to understand the mind of someone who would engage in such demonic, anti-Christ, inhumane and barbaric behavior. You have to truly be turned over to the devil himself to engage in such debauchery.

When thinking about what elements would set up an environment for someone to be trafficked, it occurs to me that being untraceable would be an attractive element. We've already discussed in previous chapters the push amongst the Sovereign Citizen and State

National cult groups to convince people to get rid of their social security numbers, their car tags, car insurance, and any number that is a traceable identification.

I would not have tied this idea to human trafficking until I did a deeper dig into this Syteria Hephzibah, who calls herself "Highly Favored Shakineh-El", her Moorish name. You will recall her from the court case of the vexatious litigant on page 69.

I've given you the whole skinny on the Moorish society; who they are and how they came to be. She is part of that group. That in and of itself does not make her a bad human, but follow all of her court cases and her arrests and you start to get a better picture of who this woman is.

It was in researching her and her tie to "Sovereign Citizen" and her claim of being Islamic that brought me to a specific talking point pushed by Sovereign Citizen's David Lester Strait concerning interesting name changes to remove yourself from the "system." In Strait's suggestions, he mentions suing people who use your name, claiming that the government, who is supposedly bankrolling your birth, can be sued by you for this. He claims you can sue them for a million dollars.

So as I was researching this woman, I found some interesting information out about her. It turns out she was arrested along with 20+ other individuals in Florida in a ring of people who created faked passports.

Here is the article from the Orlando Sentinel on February 19, 2015:

93

"In Putnam County, Syteria Hephzibah, an American citizen, received a passport with the fake name of Highly Favored Shekinah El.

She presented fake documents, including an ID called a Diplomat Nationality Identification Card.

Wendy Bashnan, the special agent leading the investigation, wouldn't name the men and women charged with defrauding the government, though Hephzibah's name came through a search of the federal court system.

Bashnan said some of the cases warrant further investigation on other allegations, including money laundering and a potential connection to human trafficking.

Hephzibah was the only citizen arrested as part of Operation Southern Wave, as the government called the law enforcement surge.

The investigation didn't reveal that any of the people arrested was a criminal kingpin, Bashnan said.

But during the arrests, law enforcement sometimes found fake driver's licenses, fake voter registration cards, fake vehicle titles and drugs.

One of the suspects, Bashnan said, is part of an $8.5 million mortgage scam.

In general, some suspects use the fake passports to avoid prosecution, Bashnan said.

'They're applying in an alias that is not theirs and they know is not theirs,' she said. 'They have purchased it.

They have stolen it. They are required to present other documentation to attest to why they are.'

Ten of the suspects had already received fake passports.

'For us who live down here in South Florida, identity theft is a very serious concern. South Florida leads the nation in the amount of identity theft cases presented in court. We feel it's a growing concern in terms of criminal activity.'

Fighting passport fraud, she said, was part of the State Department's effort to strengthen national security."

That's not all.

As I dug further on this woman, besides all the court cases, I found this very obscure listing by her in the classifieds of a small Jacksonville Florida-based black publication called the Florida Star.

As you read through this ad, a couple of things strike oddly. The cover is, "Hey don't you use my name or I will sue you." Ok, we get the point. However, upon closer inspection, I have some questions. Why is there a "Hey contact me at my personal Gmail address for more information and 'updates'." Also, what is this whole thing about a contract? What contract? Does it feel to you like there are hidden messages in this post?

Which leads me back to asking, why is this in the classifieds section of a small black publication? Who is she talking to?

PS I wonder if she will come after me for using her name in this book. I'd like to see her try, to be honest.

Circling back to my first sleuthing question, what elements are required to traffic people? There needs to be a contact, untraceable people, probably a dollar amount that is to be negotiated between the parties, and a good cover.

The dollar amount dropped in this strange, obscure post is $10,000,000. Does this seem like a normal situation to you?

Me either.

Had our good detective Wendy Bashnan not mentioned human trafficking, I might have thought I was crazy for thinking this was possibly where this could be going. I don't think I'm crazy any longer. I leave it for you to decide.

Regardless, this is exactly where you end up if you follow the whole "Sovereign Citizen" narrative through to its end. You are also invited to purchase fake license plates from David Lester Strait. I'm not sure what else he sells. He may not be as publicly forthcoming about some items. However, he has claimed that if you follow his instructions, you will never go to jail. Oddly, he keeps getting put in jail despite his claims.

Please be careful who you allow to speak into your life. That is not a nod to any letters in the alphabet that people follow. That is just good old-fashioned common sense.

"Changing Your Status"

Renouncing your citizenship is a serious decision and can have significant consequences. If you were to renounce your citizenship, you would lose the rights and privileges associated with being a U.S. Citizen, including the right to vote, work, and live in the country without immigration restrictions. You would also no longer be entitled to the protection and assistance of the U.S. government when abroad. Additionally, your nationality would change, and you would become a citizen of whichever country you choose to acquire citizenship in, if any. However, renouncing citizenship is a complex legal process. Without being a citizen of a country, you are considered to be stateless.

Becoming a citizen of a state within the United States is not a separate legal status from being a citizen of the United States. In The U.S. citizenship is granted at the federal level, and citizens are considered to be citizens of both the country and the state in which they reside. If you move to a different state, you are still a citizen of the country and now of the new state you moved to. There is no distinct process for becoming a citizen of just one state within the country.

Here are a couple of facts that destroy the whole lie behind the supposed positives of becoming a "State National." These purveyors of these delusions tell their cult followers that they are getting rid of identifiable numbers, such as the "nefarious" social security number that is actually a corporate

EIN…"you remember the thing." This is patently false.

In reality, getting rid of the social security number has nothing to do with citizenship. It's a completely different matter.

The same goes for paying taxes, which is another reason they convince people to renounce citizenship. They claim you don't have to pay taxes any longer.

Patently false!

If you continue to work in the U.S. you must have a social security number and you must pay taxes, even as a national. The Social Security number is used primarily for tax and Social Security purposes and is not specifically designed to indicate citizenship status. There is no separate, distinct number that specifically identifies a person as a U.S. citizen.

Sure, you can offload your citizenship, but it won't change this fact. Keep the Social Security number and also, don't let April 15th pass you up without paying those taxes.

What you decide about the constitutionality or lack thereof concerning paying taxes, the fact remains that even nationals must have a social security number to be gainfully employed in the United States.

I guess if you are independently wealthy and don't need an income, then you could offload your social security number. But that number doesn't get recirculated to another person. It's still attached to all of your records forever.

But the risks of having a floating social security number are this:

1. That number can now be grabbed by an illegal. This will then tie back to you.

2. That number can be used in voter fraud.

And don't forget, removing yourself from citizenship removes you from some privileges citizens have. Primarily, they cannot vote in the presidential election.

Question: Why do you think a group of people would want you to "change your status" just before an incredibly important election cycle?

Question 2: How many people do you think have been talked into "changing their status?" Do you think it is enough people to affect any election outcomes locally or nationally?

Question 3: By what percentage gap are most elections determined? 6%. That's it. Just 6%. If you can move 1% of the population this way, another 1% that way, and so forth, how might these efforts change the landscape of our constitutional republic?

We are not a corporation or a business. Each city is incorporated up under its own state's constitution. And that corporation does not take the place of state sovereignty or take it from being a sovereign constitutional state. The very first towns were incorporated, even before the constitution. Initially as colonies, they were incorporated up under the crown. Jamestown was the first. Once we won the war these towns remained incorporated except now they were so up under their individual states. The town's "corporate" needs are taken up by the state itself. All those needs, money for infrastructure, the legal entity through which to pay and receive taxes, etc, all ran through the "corporate" entity for the sake of good accounting. It's an accounting framework. Cities are not sovereign. They rely on the state. Thus corporations are formed to supply its cities. People turn 1871 into something not realizing that all towns from day 1 were always incorporated constitutionally.

The bottom line is, these corporate entities do not in any way shape, or form butt up against or contest the Constitution. They rest comfortably inside the constitution as simply the bookkeeping of the constitutional republic state by state.

DC is no different except that they are a territory instead of a state so they don't answer to a state government. They answer to Congress like all other territories for their municipal governance. The people do have some autonomy, though. They have Home Rule which is another topic and I provide a whole podcast on that on my Rumble channel. They also have some representation but not as much as the states.

These people who live there are still American citizens and fought to be represented some time back. The Revised Act of 1807 dealt with their representation, as did consequent Acts over time in their process.

Home rule exists also within the states. These are the words of one unnamed individual who is working through this process now. "There are a number of us in my community that are using the home rule pathway to incorporate our community into a township within our county. We are doing this to give ourselves more control over how our taxes are divvied up in our county, how zoning is set up, and how our existing infrastructure is managed. It is an arduous process with lots of hoops to jump through so it is progressing slowly but nevertheless, it is progressing."

(By the way, that Reitzinger woman who tells everyone she is a judge in Alaska (she's not) would REALLY like it if you send her all your money so she can build you a new currency. Not making that up.)

Capitulation Tour

According to those who have been continuously pushing the narrative of the United States being a corporation, President Trump went on what they have coined a "capitulation tour." Meaning, that President Trump traveled to several countries, and behind closed doors with the heads of these countries he showed them information in folders he brought with him of their corruption and that Trump and the military knows all.

You have likely heard Trump say, "We have it all." According to these storytellers the "all" that Trump has is the laundry list of crimes against humanity committed by all of these countries and their leaders. The storyline goes that he traveled around to expose these men, detailing their crimes to them and then forcing them to "capitulate" and basically in one form or another surrender themselves to him. Some storytellers even say they made him "king" of their countries.

Saudi Arabia

Saudi Arabia was the first stop on May 20, 2017 of a globetrotting adventure by our illustrious new president.

The narrative suggests that President Trump was celebrated by Saudi Arabian Royalty with an ancient sword dance as a symbol of complete submission of their country to him. According to this account, he is purported to be the only U.S. President in history to receive such a celebration, indicating a significant gesture of capitulation and submission of their nation to both President Trump and our "military."

Let's take a closer look into all things Saudi sword dances shall we? Initially, when I started researching this story I quickly uncovered that not only President Trump was given a sword to dance this sword dance, but so was Rex Tillerson, and Wilbur Ross. I faced resistance when I highlighted this observation, with some arguing that President Trump was presented with the most prestigious sword, a gesture typically reserved for royalty, suggesting an implicit crowning as king.

My nose was still itching about all of this, so I went digging further. Here is what I discovered.

I came across a ton of information about the Saudi sword dance called Riyadh Ardah or Saudi Ardah on Wikipedia. But my lightning quick mind told me this wouldn't fly with my readers because of our lack of trust in Wikipedia.

Instead, I went looking for an authentic site, and I found one called Arab News. Thankfully the information on this site did match up identically with Wikipedia.

According to Wikipedia, Arab News and UNESCO, (United Nations Educational Scientific and Cultural Organization) born in 1945, all agree that the Sword dances today in Saudi Arabia are purely folklore. At one time these dances were performed by tribesmen prior to heading out to war. This has passed down from generation to generation as folklore, since war is conducted much differently today than those tribal days gone by.

"Nowadays the Ardah is performed during weddings, graduations, Saudi Embassy events worldwide and Saudi National Day."

It is also performed at concerts, national festivals, and royal ceremonies held to welcome foreign dignitaries.

"The Arda is a UNESCO-listed dance that combines traditional chanting, swordplay, and rhythmic drums. It was originally used to motivate warriors and embodies loyalty and pride in Saudi culture" (Arab News).

Jumping back to UNESCO, I had never heard of this before so I went digging. This UN body is your basic world "historical society" plain and simple. It's more complex than that, but for something like this sword dance, it's basically the body that pronounced the sword dance to be a cultural icon of Saudi Arabia. And it just so happens that this sword dance made UNESCO's list in 2015, prior to President Trump being our president.

I wanted to confirm any suspicions that were lingering and went digging for this information about the type of sword Trump danced with. I found not a peep anywhere about it. All is quiet on the Western…and Eastern fronts about which sword he was handed to dance with.

I did run across the information while digging that President Trump was gifted "The Collar of the Order of Abdulaziz Al Saud." It "confers the highest rank in the Order of Abdulaziz" and "is awarded to non-Muslim heads of state.

So that confused me. Why is Saudi Arabia mantling President Trump with a "head of state" highest rank if they are not "capitulating?"

Per usual, there is an answer. "The Order of Abdulaziz Al Saud is awarded to citizens of Saudi Arabia and foreigners for meritorious service to the Kingdom. The Council of Ministers makes the nominations but the King confers awards to foreigners himself when he determines it to be appropriate." As I read further, there are different awards and different classes of these conferments, and only so many can be conferred annually. Thankfully, I found the list of those conferments. There are different categories of recipients.

1. Saudi Royalty

2. Politicians and Officials

3. Military

4. Other

And wouldn't you know it, they've listed all the folks who have been conferred these awards.

We find President Trump in list number 2, Politicians and Officials, along with these people who have also been recipients:

- Abiy Ahmed – Prime Minister of Ethiopia (9/16/2018)
- Beji Caid Essebsi – President of Tunisia (3/29/2019)

- Isaias Afwerki – President of Eritrea (9/16/2018)
- Petro Poroshenko – President of Ukraine (11/1/2017)
- Theresa May – Former Prime Minister of the United Kingdom (4/6/2017)
- Narendra Modi – Prime Minister of India, Order of Abdulaziz Al Saud (Special Class, 4/3/2016)
- Mubarak bin Mohammed Al Nahyan, Emirati official
- Jacob Zuma – President of South Africa (3/28/2016)
- Xi Jinping – President of China and General Secretary of the Chinese Communist Party, Medal of King Abdulaziz (1/20/2016)
- Enrique Peña Nieto – President of Mexico, Order of Abdulaziz Al Saud (Special Class, 1/17/2016)
- Joko Widodo – President of Indonesia, Medal of King Abdulaziz (First Class, 9/2015)
- Abdel Fattah el-Sisi – President of Egypt, Medal of King Abdulaziz (First Class; 8/2014)
- François Hollande – Former President of France, (Special Class, 12/30/2013)
- David Cameron – Former Prime Minister of the United Kingdom (11/8/2012)
- Najib Tun Razak – Former Prime Minister of Malaysia, Medal of King Abdulaziz (First Class, 1/19/2010)
- Giorgio Napolitano - Former President of Italy, Collar of the Order of Abdulaziz Al Saud (11/5/2007)
- Silvio Berlusconi – Former Prime Minister of Italy, Order of Abdulaziz Al Saud (First Class; 11/22/2009)   `
- Bashar al-Assad – President of Syria, Medal of King Abdulaziz (10/8/2009)
- Barack Obama – Former President of the United States, King Abdul Aziz Order of Merit (6/2009)
- Mohammad Al Jasser – Saudi minister, Medal of King Abdulaziz (First Class; 5/2009)
- George W. Bush – Former President of the United States, Medal of King Abdulaziz (First Class; 1/14/2008)
- Mohammed VI – King of Morocco (5/18/2007)
- Carl XVI Gustaf - King of Sweden, Grand Cross with Collar of the Order of Abdulaziz al Saud

- Shinzō Abe – Prime Minister of Japan, Order of Abdulaziz Al Saud (Special Class; 4/2007)
- Vladimir Putin – President of Russia (2/12/2007)
- Sabah Al Khalid Al Sabah – Kuwaiti royal and politician, Medal of King Abdulaziz (First Class)
- Edmond Leburton – Former Prime Minister of Belgium
- Bill Clinton – Former President of the United States
- Gyanendra of Nepal – Former King of Nepal
- Hussein bin Talal - Former King of the Hashemite Kingdom of Jordan, Collar of Abdulaziz Al Saud (1960)
- Hosni Mubarak - Former President of Egypt
- Mohammed bin Ali Aba Al Khail – Former Saudi Finance Minister, 2nd Class Sash
- Ray Mabus – Former ambassador of the United States to Saudi Arabia (4/1996)
- Shakhbout bin Nahyan bin Mubarak Al Nahyan – Former ambassador of the United Arab Emirates to Saudi Arabia, 2nd Class Sash (2/2021)
- Syed Nasir Ali Rizvi - Former Federal Minister of Pakistan for Housing and Urban development (1976)
- Halimah Yacob – President of Singapore (11/6/2019)
- Haitham bin Tariq – Sultan of Oman, (7/11/2021)
- Cyril Ramaphosa – President of South Africa (7/12/2018)
- Al-Muhtadee Billah – Crown Prince of Brunei (1/31999) (Wikipedia)

If you are like me, this all now becomes so comical that the whole thing was made into this trip being a "capitulation." I mean, did Saudi Arabia also make Xi Jinping their king? Also of note, in group 1, Saudi Royalty all got the Medal of King Abdulaziz as did Group 2 recipients, Xi, and other kings, presidents and prime ministers from several countries. It doesn't even seem as though President Trump received the highest award in the land.

Did you know that King Charles has also done the sword dance?

But still there is the question of WHY? Why was President Trump in Saudi Arabia enjoying these folklore festivals and receiving super nifty collars and things? Was he there carrying a folder of all the egregious crimes against humanity that the King and his leadership had committed?

There is no documented (or otherwise) evidence of such information anywhere. In fact, it appears to be made up out of thin air. Would you like to know the real reason he was there?

President Trump went to Saudi Arabia to sign one of the largest arms package deals ever made, helping the country to beef up protection against Iran in the region. This package amounted to $350 BILLION dollars. No wonder King Salman through President Trump a party!

So, this throws the whole "capitulation" fantasy into a tailspin. The next part of that story has President Trump going to Israel to do the same "folder reveal." Apparently, the idea that we could move our embassy into Jerusalem could only come about because the Prime Minister has to "capitulate" due to his human trafficking no-no's and the placement of our embassy in Jerusalem is how Israel is seen bowing down to President Trump.

That doesn't even make emotional sense, much less logical sense. Plus once again, there isn't an ounce of documentation to back this claim up. "We just know it happened." Says who?

But the next trip is where the most fascinating and fantastical story is said to take place in this whole tale. Unfortunately for the story crafters it hinges upon the capitulation of both Saudi Arabia and Israel, because it was supposedly the three powers put together that brought Pope Francis to heel. And here is where things really go off the rails.

The entire fantasy of Trump taking 650 planes full of gold out of the Vatican and "bankrupting the corporation" after this visit to Pope Francis in the vatican is literally based on a picture of a sour faced pope. If you have watched "The Greatest Show on Earth" with narrator Nick Alvear, he literally points to the picture the pope takes with Trump, noting the pope's awful expression, and uses that picture as the single proof that Trump read the pope's sins to him and informed the pope of Rome that he would be taking all the gold…from a picture. That's the proof.

If you'd like, please picture me putting palm to forehead and rolling my eyes.

The pope did not like Trump. And to be frank (not Francis, but frank) I don't like the pope. You likely don't either. I won't get into my beliefs about him here in a book, but seeing him come to justice would be cathartic. However, spinning this tale of President Trump when the facts are so completely different in reality is truly mind boggling. But more than that, the very idea that so many people have fallen for it without looking any of this up is baffling and telling.

I don't care if you are politically left leaning or right leaning. Confirmation bias is real, and we are addicted to and bewitched by sensationalism. Throw a sultry voice with captivating cinematography and a haunting music score and call it fact. People will fall for it every single day.

Hopefully with this writing, you will be better equipped to understand the importance of vetting any information you come in contact with.

(And hey, if you ever get to participate in a Saudi Arabian sword dance, you are not taking over their country. Just sayin'. But kick up your heels! I bet it's the experience of a lifetime.)

Conclusion

There's so much more I could say. So much more I have said and will continue to share. The questions continue to mount as more mental twists find their way into these narratives to continue to draw people through a kaleidoscope of distraction and subversion.

The thing I want you to walk away with the most, besides the knowledge of the truth, is the overall awareness that none of us are impervious to mind games.

I have a request of you. I would like you to take this information you have learned here in this book and go back and compare it to what you had come to believe is true. Did you watch "The Greatest Show on Earth" and believe it? Go watch it again through new eyes armed with information you didn't have before. What do you notice now? Anything different? Or does it still sound the same to you?

Are you captivated by the music score, the sultry voice, or the cinematography of a film? Which senses are you most attuned to? Consider this: if you were to mute the film and only read the dialogue, or if you were to remove the visuals and listen to the script in a monotone voice, how would it alter your experience? Trying this experiment can be eye-opening, revealing how much our emotions are influenced by the sensory aspects of what we consume. Often, the outcome is vastly different.

Also…

We can persist in our efforts to uncover the various ways others seek to manipulate us, constantly placing guards to protect ourselves. Yet, it is crucial to recognize that without God and the gospel in our lives—without a genuine, profound acknowledgment of our humanity and fallibility—we are susceptible to falling into traps. Even with God at the center, we may still stumble. I have, and I acknowledge that I will likely do so again.

Thankfully He is faithful to bail us out when we fall on our faces. I mean that in two ways…fall on our faces in a splat-like fashion, having to realize we are eating dirt and messed up. And…falling flat on our faces in acknowledgment that he is sovereign, He is worthy of all my adoration and praise, and He is worthy of my complete surrender and worship since He is pure love.

HE is infallible where we are not. He is our compass. When we pass everything through the Word of God, when we remain dedicated to Him as not just someone we believe in (the devil believes in him also) but someone we give Lordship to, we all have a much better shot at navigating these difficult areas with wisdom.

Along those lines, a key component of steering clear of mental subversion is the beautiful attribute of humility. Humility is a super power. It's like an oil that keeps things from sticking to us. I could spend a whole book on it. Oh wait, I'm going to. Soonish.

In the meantime, stay alert. Keep Him center. He is True North. He is the Way, the Truth, and the Life. Ask him to be your main focus and to keep your mind from manipulation by the evil that so desires to pull you from His love.

Come ask me questions. I'll likely be online at some point during my day.

God bless~

Thank you for your time.

Appendix

The Entire Organic Act of 1871 in all its glory.

CHAP. LXII.— *An Act to provide a Government for the District of Columbia.*

Be it enacted by the Senate and House of Representatives of the United States of America in Congress assembled, That all that part of the territory of the United States included within the limits of the District of Columbia be, and the same is hereby, created into a government by the name of the District of Columbia, by which name it is hereby constituted a body corporate for municipal purposes, and may contract and be contracted with, sue and be sued, plead and be impleaded, have a seal, and exercise all other powers of a municipal corporation not inconsistent with the Constitution and laws of the United States and the provisions of this act.

Sec. 2. *And be it further enacted,* That the executive power and authority in and over said District of Columbia shall be vested in a governor, who shall be appointed by the President, by and with the advice and consent of the Senate, and who shall hold his office for four years, and until his successor shall be appointed and qualified. The governor shall be a citizen of and shall have resided within said District twelve months before his appointment, and have the qualifications of an elector. He may grant pardons and respites for offenses against the laws of said District enacted by the legislative assembly thereof; he shall commission all officers who shall be elected or appointed to office under the laws of the said District enacted as aforesaid, and shall take care that the laws be faithfully executed.

Sec. 3. *And be it further enacted,* That every bill which shall have passed the council and house of delegates shall, before it becomes a law, be presented to the governor of the District of Columbia; if he approve, he shall sign it, but if not, he shall return it, with his objections, to the house in which it shall have originated, who shall enter the objections at large on their journal, and proceed to reconsider it. If, after such reconsideration, two thirds of all the members appointed or elected to the house shall agree to pass the bill, it shall be sent, together with the objections, to the other house, by which it shall likewise be reconsidered, and if approved by two thirds of all the members appointed or elected to that house, it shall become a law. But in all such cases the votes of both houses shall be determined by yeas and nays, and the names of the persons voting for and against the bill shall be entered on the journal of each house respectively. If any bill shall not be returned by the governor within ten days (Sundays excepted) after it shall have been presented to him, the same shall be a law in like manner as if he had signed it, unless the legislative assembly by their adjournment prevent its return, in which case it shall not be a law.

Sec. 4. *And be it further enacted,* That there shall be appointed by the President, by and with the advice and consent of the Senate, a secretary of said District, who shall reside therein and possess the qualification of an elector, and shall hold his office for four years, and until his successor shall be appointed and qualified; he shall record and preserve all laws and proceedings of the legislative assembly hereinafter constituted, and all the acts and proceedings of the governor in his executive department; he shall transmit one copy of the laws and journals of the legislative assembly within thirty days after the end of each session, and one copy of the executive proceedings and official correspondence semiannually, on the first days of January and July in each year, to the President of the United States, and four copies of the laws to the President of the Senate and to the Speaker of the House of Representatives, for the use of Congress; and in case of the death, removal, resignation, disability, or absence, of the governor from the District, the secretary shall be, and he is hereby, authorized and required to execute and perform all the powers and duties of the governor during such vacancy, disability, or absence, or until another governor shall be duly appointed and qualified to fill such vacancy. And in case the offices of governor and secretary shall both become vacant, the powers, duties, and emoluments of the office of governor shall devolve upon the presiding officer of the council, and in case that office shall also be vacant, upon the presiding officer of the house of delegates, until the office shall be filled by a new appointment.

Sec. 5. *And be it further enacted,* That legislative power and authority in said District shall be vested in a legislative assembly as hereinafter provided. The assembly shall consist of a council and house of delegates. The council shall consist of eleven members, of whom two shall be residents of the city of Georgetown, and two residents of the county outside of the cities of Washington and Georgetown, who shall be appointed by the President, by and with the advice and consent of the Senate, who shall have the qualification of voters as hereinafter prescribed, five of whom shall be first appointed for the term of one year, and six for the period of two years, provided that all subsequent appointments shall be for the term of two years. The house of delegates shall consist of twenty-two members, possessing the same qualifications as prescribed for the members of the council, whose term of service shall continue one year. An apportionment shall be made, as nearly equal as practicable, into eleven districts for the appointment of the council, and into twenty-two districts for the election of delegates, giving to each section of the District representation in the ratio of its population as nearly as may be. And the members of the council and of the house of delegates shall reside in and be inhabitants of the districts from which they are appointed or elected, respectively. For the purposes of the first election to be held under this act, the governor and judges of the supreme court of the District of Columbia shall designate the districts for members of the house of delegates, appoint a board of registration and persons to superintend the election and the returns thereof, prescribe the time, places, and manner of conducting such election, and make all needful rules and regulations for carrying into effect the provisions of this act not otherwise herein provided for : *Provided*, That the first election shall be held within sixty days from the passage of this act. In the first and all subsequent elections the persons having the highest number of legal votes for the house of delegates, respectively, shall be declared by the governor duly elected members of said house. In case two or more persons voted for shall have an equal number of votes for the same office, or if a vacancy shall occur in the house of delegates, the governor shall order a new election. And the persons thus appointed and elected to the legislative assembly shall meet at such time and at such place within the District as the governor shall appoint; but thereafter the time, place, and manner of holding and conducting all elections by the people, and the formation of the districts for members of the council and house of delegates, shall be prescribed by law, as well as the day of the commencement of the regular sessions of the legislative assembly : *Provided*, That no session in any one year shall exceed the term of sixty days, except the first session, which may continue one hundred days.

SEC. 6. *And be it further enacted*, That the legislative assembly shall have power to divide that portion of the District not included in the corporate limits of Washington or Georgetown into townships, not exceeding three, and create township officers, and prescribe the duties thereof; but all township officers shall be elected by the people of the townships respectively.

SEC. 7. *And be it further enacted*, That all male citizens of the United States, above the age of twenty-one years, who shall have been actual residents of said District for three months prior to the passage of this act, except such as are non compos mentis and persons convicted of infamous crimes, shall be entitled to vote at said election, in the election district or precinct in which he shall then reside, and shall have so resided for thirty days immediately preceding said election, and shall be eligible to any office within the said District, and for all subsequent elections twelve months' prior residence shall be required to constitute a voter; but the legislative assembly shall have no right to abridge or limit the right of suffrage.

SEC. 8. *And be it further enacted*, That no person who has been or hereafter shall be convicted of bribery, perjury, or other infamous crime, nor any person who has been or may be a collector or holder of public moneys who shall not have accounted for and paid over, upon final judgment duly recovered according to law, all such moneys due from him, shall be eligible to the legislative assembly or to any office of profit or trust in said District.

SEC. 9. *And be it further enacted*, That members of the legislative assembly, before they enter upon their official duties, shall take and subscribe the following oath or affirmation: "I do solemnly swear (or affirm) that I will support the Constitution of the United States, and will faithfully discharge the duties of the office upon which I am about to enter; and that I have not knowingly or intentionally paid or contributed anything, or made any promise in the nature of a bribe, to directly or indirectly influence any vote at the election at which I was chosen to fill the said office, and have not accepted, nor will I accept, or receive, directly or indirectly, any money or other valuable thing for any vote or influence that I may give or withhold on any bill, resolution, or appropriation, or for any other official act." Any member who shall refuse to take the oath herein prescribed shall forfeit his office, and every person who shall be convicted of having sworn falsely to or of violating his said oath shall forfeit his office and be disqualified thereafter from holding any office of profit or trust in said District, and shall be

117

deemed guilty of perjury, and upon conviction shall be punished accordingly.

Sec. 10. *And be it further enacted,* That a majority of the legislative assembly appointed or elected to each house shall constitute a quorum. The house of delegates shall be the judge of the election returns and qualifications of its members. Each house shall determine the rules of its proceedings, and shall choose its own officers. The governor shall call the council to order at the opening of each new assembly; and the secretary of the District shall call the house of delegates to order at the opening of each new legislative assembly, and shall preside over it until a temporary presiding officer shall have been chosen and shall have taken his seat. No member shall be expelled by either house except by a vote of two thirds of all the members appointed or elected to that house. Each house may punish by imprisonment any person not a member who shall be guilty of disrespect to the house by disorderly or contemptuous behavior in its presence; but no such imprisonment shall extend beyond twenty-four hours at one time. Neither house shall, without the consent of the other, adjourn for more than two days, or to any other place than that in which such house shall be sitting. At the request of any member the yeas and nays shall be taken upon any question and entered upon the journal.

Sec. 11. *And be it further enacted,* That bills may originate in either house, but may be altered, amended, or rejected by the other; and on the final passage of all bills the vote shall be by yeas and nays upon each bill separately, and shall be entered upon the journal, and no bill shall become a law without the concurrence of a majority of the members elected to each house.

Sec. 12. *And be it further enacted,* That every bill shall be read at large on three different days in each house. No act shall embrace more than one subject, and that shall be expressed in its title; but if any subject shall be embraced in an act which shall not be expressed in the title, such act shall be void only as to so much thereof as shall not be so expressed in the title; and no act of the legislative assembly shall take effect until thirty days after its passage, unless, in case of emergency, (which emergency shall be expressed in the preamble or body of the act,) the legislative assembly shall by a vote of two thirds of all the members appointed or elected to each house otherwise direct.

Sec. 13. *And be it further enacted,* That no money shall be drawn from the treasury of the District, except in pursuance of an appropriation made by law, and no bill making appropriations for the pay or salaries of the officers of the District government shall contain any provisions on any other subject.

Sec. 14. *And be it further enacted,* That each legislative assembly shall provide for all the appropriations necessary for the ordinary and contingent expenses of the government of the District until the expiration of the first fiscal quarter after the adjournment of the next regular session, the aggregate amount of which shall not be increased without a vote of two thirds of the members elected or appointed to each house as herein provided, nor exceed the amount of revenue authorized by law to be raised in such time, and all appropriations, general or special, requiring money to be paid out of the District treasury, from funds belonging to the District, shall end with such fiscal quarter; and no debt, by which the aggregate debt of the District shall exceed five per cent. of the assessed property of the District, shall be contracted, unless the law authorizing the same shall at a general election have been submitted to the people and have received a majority of the votes cast for members of the legislative assembly at such election. The legislative assembly shall provide for the publication of said law in at least two newspapers in the District for three months, at least, before the vote of every hundred dollars of the cash value thereof; but special taxes may be levied in particular sections, wards, or districts for their particular local improvements; nor shall said territorial government have power to borrow money or issue stock or bonds for any object whatever, unless specially authorized by an act of the legislative assembly, passed by a vote of two thirds of the entire number of the members of each branch thereof, but said debt in no case to exceed five per centum of the assessed value of the property of said District, unless authorized by a vote of the people, as hereinafter [hereinbefore] provided.

SEC. 21. And be it further enacted, That the property of that portion of the District not included in the corporations of Washington or Georgetown shall not be taxed for the purposes either of improving the streets, alleys, public squares, or other public property of the said cities, or either of them, nor for any other expenditure of a local nature, for the exclusive benefit of said cities, or either of them, nor for the payment of any debt heretofore contracted, or that may hereafter be contracted by either of said cities while remaining under a municipal government not coextensive with the District.

SEC. 22. And be it further enacted, That the property within the corporate limits of Georgetown shall not be taxed for the payment of any debt heretofore or hereafter to be contracted by the corporation of Washington, nor shall the property within the corporate limits of Washington be taxed for the payment of any debt heretofore or hereafter to be contracted by the corporation of Georgetown; and so long as said cities shall remain under distinct municipal governments, the property within the corporate limits of either of said cities shall not be taxed for the local benefit of the other; nor shall said cities, or either of them, be taxed for the exclusive benefit of the county outside of the limits thereof: Provided, That the legislative assembly may make appropriations for the repair of roads, or for the construction or repair of bridges outside the limits of said cities.

SEC. 23. And be it further enacted, That it shall be the duty of said legislative assembly to maintain a system of free schools for the education of the youth of said District, and all moneys raised by general taxation or arising from donations by Congress, or from other sources, except by bequest or devise, for school purposes, shall be appropriated for the equal benefit of all the youths of said District between certain ages, to be defined by law.

SEC. 24. And be it further enacted, That the said legislative assembly shall have power to provide for the appointment of as many justices of the peace and notaries public for said District as may be deemed necessary, to define their jurisdiction and prescribe their duties; but justices of the peace shall not have jurisdiction of any controversy in which the title of land may be in dispute, or in which the debt or sum claimed shall exceed one hundred dollars: Provided, however, That all justices of the peace and notaries public now in commission shall continue in office till their present commissions expire, unless sooner removed pursuant to existing laws.

SEC. 25. And be it further enacted, That the judicial courts of said District shall remain as now organized until abolished or changed by act of Congress; but such legislative assembly shall have power to pass laws modifying the practice thereof, and conferring such additional jurisdiction as may be necessary to the due execution and enforcement of the laws of said District.

SEC. 26. And be it further enacted, That there shall be appointed by the President of the United States, by and with the advice and consent of the Senate, a board of health for said District, to consist of five persons, whose duty it shall be to declare what shall be deemed nuisances injurious to health, and to provide for the removal thereof; to make and enforce regulations to prevent domestic animals from running at large in the cities of Washington and Georgetown; to prevent the sale of unwholesome food in said cities; and to perform such other duties as shall be imposed upon said board by the legislative assembly.

Sec. 27. *And be it further enacted,* That the offices and duties of register of wills, recorder of deeds, United States attorney, and United States marshal for said District shall remain as under existing laws till modified by act of Congress; but said legislative assembly shall have power to impose such additional duties upon said officers, respectively, as may be necessary to the due enforcement of the laws of said District.

Sec. 28. *And be it further enacted,* That the said legislative assembly shall have power to create by general law, modify, repeal, or amend within said District, corporations aggregate for religious, charitable, educational, industrial, or commercial purposes, and to define their powers and liabilities: *Provided,* That the powers of corporations so created shall be limited to the District of Columbia.

Sec. 29. *And be it further enacted,* That the legislative assembly shall define by law who shall be entitled to relief as paupers in said District, and shall provide by law for the support and maintenance of such paupers, and for that purpose shall raise the money necessary by taxation.

Sec. 30. *And be it further enacted,* That the legislative assembly shall have power to provide by law for the election or appointment of such ministerial officers as may be deemed necessary to carry into effect the laws of said District, to prescribe their duties, their terms of office, and the rate and manner of their compensation.

Sec. 31. *And be it further enacted,* That the governor, secretary, and other officers to be appointed pursuant to this act, shall, before they act as such, respectively, take and subscribe an oath or affirmation before a judge of the supreme court of the District of Columbia, or some justice of the peace in the limits of said District, duly authorized to administer oaths or affirmations by the laws now in force therein, or before the Chief Justice or some associate justice of the Supreme Court of the United States, to support the Constitution of the United States, and faithfully to discharge the duties of their respective offices; which said oaths, when so taken, shall be certified by the person before whom the same shall have been taken; and such certificates shall be received and recorded by the said secretary among the executive proceedings; and all civil officers in said District, before they act as such, shall take and subscribe a like oath or affirmation before the said governor or secretary, or some judge or justice of the peace of the District, who may be duly commissioned and qualified, or before the Chief Justice of the Supreme Court of the United States, which said oath or affirmation shall be certified and transmitted by the person administering the same to the secretary, to be by him recorded as aforesaid; and afterward the like oath or affirmation shall be taken and subscribed, certified and recorded in such manner and form as may be prescribed by law.

Sec. 32. *And be it further enacted,* That the governor shall receive an annual salary of three thousand dollars; and the secretary shall receive an annual salary of two thousand dollars, and that the said salaries shall be paid quarter-yearly, from the dates of the respective appointments, at the treasury of the United States; but no payment shall be made until said officers shall have entered upon the duties of their respective appointments. The members of the legislative assembly shall be entitled to receive four dollars each per day during their actual attendance at the session thereof, and an additional allowance of four dollars per day shall be paid to the presiding officer of each house for each day he shall so preside. And a chief clerk, one assistant clerk, one engrossing and one enrolling clerk, and a sergeant-at-arms may be chosen for each house;

and the chief clerk shall receive four dollars per day, and the said other officers three dollars per day, during the session of the legislative assembly: *Provided*, That there shall be but one session of the legislative assembly annually, unless, on an extraordinary occasion, the governor shall think proper to call the legislative assembly together. And the governor and secretary of the District shall, in the disbursement of all moneys appropriated by Congress and intrusted to them, be governed solely by the instructions of the Secretary of the Treasury of the United States, and shall semiannually account to the said Secretary for the manner in which the aforesaid moneys shall have been expended; and no expenditure shall be made by the said legislative assembly of funds appropriated by Congress, for objects not especially authorized by acts of Congress making the appropriations, nor beyond the sums thus appropriated for such objects.

SEC. 33. *And be it further enacted,* That the legislative assembly of the District of Columbia shall hold its first session at such time and place in said District as the governor thereof shall appoint and direct.

SEC. 34. *And be it further enacted,* That a delegate to the House of Representatives of the United States, to serve for the term of two years, who shall be a citizen of the United States and of the District of Columbia, and shall have the qualifications of a voter, may be elected by the voters qualified to elect members of the legislative assembly, who shall be entitled to the same rights and privileges as are exercised and enjoyed by the delegates from the several Territories of the United States to the House of Representatives, and shall also be a member of the committee for the District of Columbia; but the delegate first elected shall hold his seat only during the term of the Congress to which he shall be elected. The first election shall be held at the time and places and be conducted in such manner as the elections for members of the House of Representatives are conducted; and at all subsequent elections the time and places and the manner of holding the elections shall be prescribed by law. The person having the greatest number of legal votes shall be declared by the governor to be duly elected, and a certificate thereof shall be given accordingly; and the Constitution and all the laws of the United States, which are not locally inapplicable, shall have the same force and effect within the said District of Columbia as elsewhere within the United States.

SEC. 35. *And be it further enacted,* That all officers to be appointed by the President of the United States, by and with the advice and consent of the Senate, for the District of Columbia, who, by virtue of the provisions of any law now existing, or which may be enacted by Congress, are required to give security for moneys that may be intrusted to them for disbursement, shall give such security at such time and in such manner as the Secretary of the Treasury may prescribe.

SEC. 36. *And be it further enacted,* That there shall be a valuation taken in the District of Columbia of all real estate belonging to the United States in said District, except the public buildings, and the grounds which have been dedicated to the public use as parks and squares, at least once in five years, and return thereof shall be made by the governor to the President of the Senate and Speaker of the House of Representatives on the first day of the session of Congress held after such valuation shall be taken, and the aggregate of the valuation of private property in said District, whenever made by the authority of the legislative assembly, shall be reported to Congress by the governor: *Provided,* That all valuations of property belonging to the United States shall be made by such persons as the Secretary of the Interior shall appoint, and under such regulations as he shall prescribe.

SEC. 37. *And be it further enacted,* That there shall be in the District of Columbia a board of public works, to consist of the governor, who

121

shall be president of said board; four persons, to be appointed by the President of the United States, by and with the advice and consent of the Senate, one of whom shall be a civil engineer, and the others citizens and residents of the District, having the qualifications of an elector therein; one of said board shall be a citizen and resident of Georgetown, and one of said board shall be a citizen and resident of the county outside of the cities of Washington and Georgetown. They shall hold office for the term of four years, unless sooner removed by the President of the United States. The board of public works shall have entire control of and make all regulations which they shall deem necessary for keeping in repair the streets, avenues, alleys, and sewers of the city, and all other works which may be intrusted to their charge by the legislative assembly or Congress. They shall disburse upon their warrant all moneys appropriated by the United States, or the District of Columbia, or collected from property-holders, in pursuance of law, for the improvement of streets, avenues, alleys, and sewers, and roads and bridges, and shall assess in such manner as shall be prescribed by law, upon the property adjoining and to be specially benefited by the improvements authorized by law and made by them, a reasonable proportion of the cost of the improvement, not exceeding one third of such cost, which sum shall be collected as all other taxes are collected. They shall make all necessary regulations respecting the construction of private buildings in the District of Columbia, subject to the supervision of the legislative assembly. All contracts made by the said board of public works shall be in writing, and shall be signed by the parties making the same, and a copy thereof shall be filed in the office of the secretary of the District; and said board of public works shall have no power to make contracts to bind said District to the payment of any sums of money except in pursuance of appropriations made by law, and not until such appropriations shall have been made. All contracts made by said board in which any member of said board shall be personally interested shall be void, and no payment shall be made thereon by said District or any officers thereof. On or before the first Monday in November of each year, they shall submit to each branch of the legislative assembly a report of their transactions during the preceding year, and also furnish duplicates of the same to the governor, to be by him laid before the President of the United States for transmission to the two houses of Congress; and shall be paid the sum of two thousand five hundred dollars each annually.

Sec. 38. *And be it further enacted,* That the officers herein provided for, who shall be appointed by the President, by and with the advice and consent of the Senate, shall be paid by the United States by appropriations to be made by law as hereinbefore provided; and all other officers of said District provided for by this act shall be paid by the District: *Provided,* That no salary shall be paid to the governor as a member of the board of public works in addition to his salary as governor, nor shall any officer of the army appointed upon the board of public works receive any increase of pay for such service.

Sec. 39. *And be it further enacted,* That if, at any election hereafter held in the District of Columbia, any person shall knowingly personate and vote, or attempt to vote, in the name of any other person, whether living, dead, or fictitious, or vote more than once at the same election for any candidate for the same office, or vote at a place where he may not be entitled to vote, or vote without having a lawful right to vote, or do any unlawful act to secure a right or opportunity to vote for himself or any other person, or by force, threats, menace, or intimidation, bribery, reward, or offer, or promise thereof, or otherwise unlawfully prevent any qualified voter of the District of Columbia from freely exercising the right of suffrage, or by any such means induce any voter to refuse to exercise such right, or compel or induce, by any such means or otherwise, any officer of any election in said District to receive a vote from a person not legally qualified or entitled to vote; or interfere in any manner with any officer of said elections in the discharge of his duties; or by any unlawful means induce any officer of an election, or officer whose duty it is to ascertain, announce, or declare the result of any such election, or give or make any certificate, document, or evidence in relation thereto, to violate or refuse to comply with his duty, or any law regulating the same; or knowingly and wilfully receive the vote of any person not entitled to vote, or refuse to receive the vote of any person entitled to vote; or aid, counsel, procure, or advise any such voter, person, or officer to do any act hereby made a crime, or to omit to do any duty the omission of which is hereby made a crime, or attempt to do so, every such person shall be deemed guilty of a crime, and shall for such crime be liable to prosecution in any court of the United States of competent jurisdiction, and on conviction thereof shall be punished by a fine not exceeding five hundred dollars, or by imprisonment for a term not exceeding three years, or both, in the discretion of the court, and shall pay the costs of prosecution.

Sec. 40. *And be it further enacted*, That the charters of the cities of Washington and Georgetown shall be repealed on and after the first day of June, A. D. eighteen hundred and seventy-one, and all offices of said corporations abolished at that date; the levy court of the District of Columbia and all offices connected therewith shall be abolished on and after said first day of June, A. D. eighteen hundred and seventy-one; but all laws and ordinances of said cities, respectively, and of said levy court, not inconsistent with this act, shall remain in full force until modified or repealed by Congress or the legislative assembly of said District; that portion of said District included within the present limits of the city of Washington shall continue to be known as the city of Washington; and that portion of said District included within the limits of the city of Georgetown shall continue to be known as the city of Georgetown; and the legislative assembly shall have power to levy a special tax upon property, except the property of the government of the United States, within the city of Washington for the payment of the debts of said city; and upon property, except the property of the government of the United States, within the limits of the city of Georgetown for the payment of the debts of said city; and upon property, except the property of the government of the United States, within said District not included within the limits of either of said cities to pay any debts owing by that portion of said District: *Provided*, That the charters of said cities severally, and the powers of said levy court, shall be continued for the following purposes, to wit: For the collection of all sums of money due to said cities, respectively, or to said levy court; for the enforcement of all contracts made by said cities, respectively, or by said levy court, and all taxes, heretofore assessed, remaining unpaid; for the collection of all just claims against said cities, respectively, or against said levy court; for the enforcement of all legal contracts against said cities, respectively, or against said levy court, until the affairs of said cities, respectively, and of said levy court, shall have been fully closed; and no suit in favor of or against said corporations, or either of them, shall abate by reason of the passage of this act, but the same shall be prosecuted to final judgment as if this act had not been passed.

Sec. 41. *And be it further enacted*, That there shall be no election holden for mayor or members of the common council of the city of Georgetown prior to the first day of June, eighteen hundred and seventy-one, but the present mayor and common council of said city shall hold their offices until said first day of June next. No taxes for general purposes shall hereafter be assessed by the municipal authorities of the cities of Washington or Georgetown, or by said levy court. And upon the repeal of the charters of the cities of Washington and Georgetown, officer of any election in said District to receive a vote from a person not legally qualified or entitled to vote; or interfere in any manner with any officer of said elections in the discharge of his duties; or by any unlawful means induce any officer of an election, or officer whose duty it is to ascertain, announce, or declare the result of any such election, or give or make any certificate, document, or evidence in relation thereto, to violate or refuse to comply with his duty, or any law regulating the same; or knowingly and willfully receive the vote of any person not entitled to vote, or refuse to receive the vote of any person entitled to vote; or aid, counsel, procure, or advise any such voter, person, or officer to do any act hereby made a crime, or to omit to do any duty the omission of which is hereby made a crime, or attempt to do so, every such person shall be deemed guilty of a crime, and shall for such crime be liable to prosecution in any court of the United States of competent jurisdiction, and on conviction thereof shall be punished by a fine not exceeding five hundred dollars, or by imprisonment for a term not exceeding three years, or both, in the discretion of the court, and shall pay the costs of prosecution.

Sec. 40. *And be it further enacted*, That the charters of the cities of Washington and Georgetown shall be repealed on and after the first day of June, A. D. eighteen hundred and seventy-one, and all offices of said corporations abolished at that date; the levy court of the District of Columbia and all offices connected therewith shall be abolished on and after said first day of June, A. D. eighteen hundred and seventy-one; but all laws and ordinances of said cities, respectively, and of said levy court, not inconsistent with this act, shall remain in full force until modified or repealed by Congress or the legislative assembly of said District; that portion of said District included within the present limits of the city of Washington shall continue to be known as the city of Washington; and that portion of said District included within the limits of the city of Georgetown shall continue to be known as the city of Georgetown; and the legislative assembly shall have power to levy a special tax upon property, except the property of the government of the United States, within the city of Washington for the payment of the debts of said city; and upon property, except the property of the government of the United States, within the limits of the city of Georgetown for the payment of the debts of said city; and upon property, except the property of the government of the United States, within said District not included within the limits of either of said cities to pay any debts owing by that portion of said District: *Provided*, That the charters of said cities severally, and the powers of said levy court, shall be continued for the following purposes, to wit: For the collection of all sums of money due to said cities, respectively, or to said levy court; for the enforcement of all contracts made by said cities, respectively, or by said levy court, and all taxes, heretofore assessed, remaining unpaid; for the collection of all just claims against said cities, respectively, or against said levy court; for the enforcement of all legal contracts against said cities, respectively, or against said levy court, until the affairs of said cities, respectively, and of said levy court, shall have been fully closed; and no suit in favor of or against said corporations, or either of them, shall abate by reason of the passage of this act, but the same shall be prosecuted to final judgment as if this act had not been passed.

Sec. 41. *And be it further enacted*, That there shall be no election holden for mayor or members of the common council of the city of Georgetown prior to the first day of June, eighteen hundred and seventy-one, but the present mayor and common council of said city shall hold their offices until said first day of June next. No taxes for general purposes shall hereafter be assessed by the municipal authorities of the cities of Washington or Georgetown, or by said levy court. And upon the repeal of the charters of the cities of Washington and Georgetown,

124

the District of Columbia be, and is hereby, declared to be the successor of said corporations, and all the property of said corporations, and of the county of Washington, shall become vested in the said District of Columbia, and all fines, penalties, costs, and forfeitures, which are now by law made payable to said cities, respectively, or said levy court, shall be paid to said District of Columbia, and the salaries of the judge and clerk of the police court, the compensation of the deputy clerk and bailiffs of said police court, and of the marshall of the District of Columbia shall be paid by said District: *Provided,* That the moneys collected upon the judgements of said police court, or so much thereof as may be necessary, shall be applied to the payment of the salaries of the judge and other officers of said court, and to the payment of the necessary expenses thereof, and any surplus remaining after paying the salaries, comp tion, and expenses aforesaid, shall be paid into the treasury of the District at the end of every quarter.

APPROVED, February 21, 1871.

District of Columbia to be the successor of the cities of Washington and Georgetown, &c.

Fines and costs.

Salaries of judge and other officers of police court.

Surplus to be paid into the treasury.

Article of Incorporation of the United States
Corporation Company (6 photos)

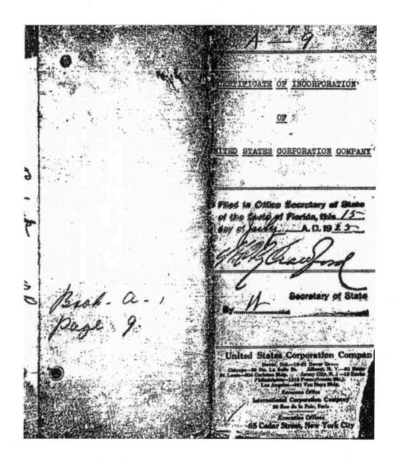

CERTIFICATE OF INCORPORATION

OF

UNITED STATES CORPORATION COMPANY

-----ooOoo-----

1. The name of the corporation is

UNITED STATES CORPORATION COMPANY.

2. The nature of the business and the objects and
purposes proposed to be transacted, promoted or carried on
by the corporation are as follows:

To prepare or cause to be prepared and procure to
be filed, recorded, registered, published, issued or granted,
in accordance with law, articles or certificates of incorporation, applications for letters patent, charters and other
instruments relating to the incorporation and organization
of corporations and joint stock companies.

To prepare or cause to be prepared and procure to
be filed, recorded, registered, published, issued or granted,
certificates, reports, statements, applications for licenses
to do business or other instruments in relation to domestic
and foreign corporations, companies or associations.

To provide and maintain domiciliary and other offices and facilities for corporations, companies and associations, and to act as agent in charge thereof and upon whom
process against or any official notices to any such corporation, company or association may be served or given, and for
any other lawful purpose.

To act as the fiscal or transfer agent of, or re-
gistrar of the stock or securities issued by any public or
private corporation; and in such capacity to receive and dis-

127

burse money, to transfer, register, countersign, issue and deliver certificates of stock, bonds or other evidences of indebtedness, and to act as agent of any corporation, foreign or domestic, for any lawful purpose.

To carry on the business of an appraisal and audit company and in connection therewith to make examinations and appraisals of the business and property of corporations and individuals, to examine and audit their books and accounts, and to make reports and certificates in respect thereof.

To publish and deal in books, periodicals, pamphlets, legal forms and blanks of all kinds.

To acquire by purchase or otherwise, and to hold for investment or otherwise to use, sell, lease or dispose of real estate and real property, and any interest, estate or rights therein.

To acquire by purchase, subscription or otherwise and to hold for investment or otherwise, and to use, sell or dispose of shares of stock, bonds or any other obligations or securities of any corporation, domestic or foreign; to aid in any manner any corporation whose shares of stock, bonds or other obligations are held or in any manner guaranteed by the company, or in which the company is in any way interested; and to do any other acts or things for the preservation, protection, improvement or enhancement of the value of any such shares of stock, bonds or other obligations, or to do any acts or things designed for any such purpose; and while owner of any such shares of stock, bonds or other obligations, to exercise all the rights, powers and privileges of ownership thereof, and to exercise any and all voting powers thereon.

To acquire by purchase or otherwise, and to hold, own, use, grant licenses in respect to, or otherwise turn to account or dispose of any copyrights, trademarks, inventions patent rights and letters patent of the United States or of any other country.

The business of the corporation is from time to time to do any one or more of the acts and things herein set forth; and it may conduct business in the State of Florida, other states, the District of Columbia, the territories and colonies of the United States and in foreign countries, have one or more offices out of the State of Florida, and hold, purchase, mortgage and convey real and personal property within or without of the State of Florida.

3. The maximum number of shares which this corporation is authorized to have outstanding at any time is ONE HUNDRED (100), each of which shares shall have a par value of ONE HUNDRED DOLLARS ($100.)

4. The amount of capital with which the corporation will begin business is FIVE HUNDRED DOLLARS ($500.)

5. The corporation is to have perpetual existence.

6. The principal office of the corporation shall be located in the Centennial Building, Tallahassee, Leon County.

7. The number of directors shall be three (3)

8. The names of the directors who shall hold office for the first year of the corporation's existence, or until their successors are elected and have qualified and their post-office addresses are as follows:

NAMES	POST-OFFICE ADDRESSES
HARRY O. COUGHLAN	150 BROADWAY, NEW YORK, N. Y.
SAMUEL B. HOWARD	150 BROADWAY, NEW YORK, N. Y.
ARTHUR W. BRITTON	150 BROADWAY, NEW YORK, N.Y.

9. The names and post-office addresses of the subscribers of this certificate and the number of shares of stock which each agrees to take are as follows:

NAMES	POST-OFFICE ADDRESSES	NO. OF SHARES
LOUIS H. GUNTHER	150 BROADWAY, NEW YORK, N.Y.	2
SAMUEL B. HOWARD	150 BROADWAY, NEW YORK, N.Y.	2
ARTHUR W. BRITTON	150 BROADWAY, NEW YORK, N.Y.	1

10. The directors and stockholders shall have power to hold their meetings and to have one or more offices and to keep the books of the corporation (except the original or duplicate stock ledger) outside of the State of Florida, at such place or places as from time to time may be designated by the By-Laws or by resolution of the Board.

The directors shall also have power, without the assent or vote of the stockholders, to make and alter by-laws of the corporation; to fix the times for the declaration and payment of dividends; and to fix and vary the amount to be reserved as working capital; to determine the use and disposition of any surplus or net profits over and above the capital stock paid in, and in their discretion the directors may use and apply any such surplus or accumulated profits in purchasing or acquiring the bonds or other obligations or shares of the capital stock of the corporation to such extent and in such manner and upon such terms as the directors shall deem expedient; but shares of such capital stock so purchased or acquired may be resold unless such shares shall have been retired for the purpose of decreasing the corporation's capital stock as provided by law.

WE, THE UNDERSIGNED, being each of the original
ubscribers to capital stock hereinbefore named, do hereby
associate for the purpose of establishing a corporation pursuant to the Corporation Law, State of Florida, 1925.

WITNESS our hands and seals this 7th day of July
.'25.

IN PRESENCE OF:

(L.S.)
(L.S.)
(L.S.)

STATE OF NEW YORK, COUNTY OF NEW YORK, July 7th,
A. D., 1925, personally appeared before me, a Notary Public
in and for New York County, duly authorized to take acknow-
ledgments, LOUIS H. GUNTHER, SAMUEL R. HOWARD and ARTHUR
W. BRITTON, to me known and known to me to be the persons
described in and who executed the foregoing instrument, who
each acknowledged to me that he executed the same freely and
voluntarily as and for his act and deed for the uses and
purposes therein expressed.

WITNESS my hand and official seal the day and year
in this certificate first above written, at New York, New
York County, New York.

Samuel C. Wood,
notary Public
my commission expire.
march 30, 1927.

131

Remaining 8 pages of Court Case 20-40375-KKS

U.S.C. § 105, a court may issue any order or take any action "necessary or appropriate to enforce or implement court orders or rules, or to prevent an abuse of the process."[18]

The Involuntary Petition was filed in bad faith.

The documented entitled "*Universal and International Humanitarian Declaration for Common Law Prejudgment Writ of Personal Replevin*" attached to the Involuntary Petition is the very document that formed the foundation of the suit dismissed with prejudice by the District Court for the Middle District of Florida in 2017 as vexatious and patently frivolous.[18] Hephzibah a/k/a Shekinah-El knowingly filed the Involuntary Petition based on that document for the improper purpose of harassing the same federal and state officials whom she and Gullett have previously named as defendants.

Allowing such patently frivolous claims to continue would harm the integrity of the judicial system.

---

[18] 11 U.S.C. § 105(a) (2020); *cf. Marrama v. Citizens of Bank of Mass.*, 549 U.S. 365, 375–76 (2007) (stating that even if § 105(a) had not been enacted, the bankruptcy court's inherent authority permits sanctions for "abusive litigation practice").
[19] Doc. 1-7; Doc. 38, pp. 2–3; *Gullett-El*, 2017 WL 10861313, at *1, *4.

7

132

The Court may properly enjoin Hephzibah a/k/a Shekinah-El as a vexatious litigant.

Hephzibah a/k/a Shekinah-El has a history of filing duplicative, vexatious, and frivolous lawsuits, including the Involuntary Petition commencing this case. The Court has the responsibility and authority to prevent vexatious litigants, such as Hephzibah a/k/a Shekinah-El, "from unnecessarily encroaching on the judicial machinery as needed by others."[20] Because Hephzibah a/k/a Shekinah-El has demonstrated an intent to continue her abusive litigation history, sanctions, including limiting future access to the judicial system, are warranted.[21]

The Eleventh Circuit has long recognized a court's inherent ability to issue injunctions against abusive and vexatious litigants.[22] "Such injunctions may be appropriate to protect both the court and its staff, as well as the right of all litigants in the federal system."[23] Courts may enjoin not only the abusive litigant, but *any* party working in concert or at

---

[20] *Procup v. Strickland*, 792 F.2d 1069, 1074 (11th Cir. 1986) (en banc) (per curiam); *accord Law*, 571 U.S. at 420–21 (stating that a bankruptcy court has the inherent and statutory power of § 105(a) to sanction abusive litigation tactics).

[21] *See Silva v. Swift*, No. 4:19-cv-286-RH/MJF, 2020 WL 3523400, at *7–8 (N.D. Fla. June 1, 2020), adopted by No. 4:19-cv-286-RH/MJF, 2020 WL 3287884 (N.D. Fla. June 18, 2020); *see also Safir v. U.S. Lines, Inc.*, 792 F.2d 19, 25 ("Ultimately, the question the court must answer is whether a litigant who has a history of vexatious litigation is likely to continue to abuse the judicial process and harass other parties.").

[22] *See Procup*, 792 F.2d at 1071–74.

[23] *Barash v. Kates*, 586 F. Supp. 2d 1323, 1325 (S.D. Fla. 2008) (citing *Procup*, 792 F.2d at 1071–72).

8

the behest of the litigant.[24] "The only restriction this Circuit has placed upon injunctions designed to protect against abusive and vexatious litigation is that a litigant cannot be 'completely foreclosed from *any* access to the court.'"[25] The Eleventh Circuit has upheld injunctions, commonly referred to as "*Martin-Trigona* Injunctions," that impose prefiling screening procedures on vexatious litigants.[26] Having determined that Hephzibah a/k/a Shekinah-El filed the Involuntary Petition in bad faith and is a vexatious litigant, the Court may properly issue a *Martin-Trigona* Injunction to prevent further abuse of the judicial system.[27]

---

[24] *Id.* at 1326 (citing *Martin-Trigona v. Shaw*, 986 F.2d 1384, 1387–89 (11th Cir. 1993) (per curiam)).

[25] *Martin-Trigona*, 986 F.2d at 1387 (quoting *Procup*, 792 F.2d at 1074 (emphasis in original)).

[26] *Law Watkins v. Dubreuil*, 820 Fed App'x 940 (11th Cir. 2020) (upholding injunction prohibiting litigant from filing new lawsuit without prior court approval); *Martin-Trigona*, 986 F.2d at 1387 (upholding an injunction that prohibited litigant "from filing or attempting to initiate any new lawsuit in any federal court in the United States . . . without first obtaining leave of that federal court."); *Copeland v. Green*, 949 F.2d 390 (11th Cir. 1991) (upholding the prefiling requirement that the clerk must submit the litigant's papers to the judge for approval); *Cofield v. Ala. Public Serv. Com'n*, 936 F.2d 512, 518 (11th Cir. 1991) (upholding injunction requiring the plaintiff "to send all pleadings to a judge for prefiling approval").

[27] *See Carroll v. Abide (In re Carroll)*, 850 F.3d 811 (5th Cir. 2017) (affirming a bankruptcy court's decision to issue a pre-filing injunction pursuant to its inherent authority and statutory powers under 28 U.S.C. § 1651(a) and 11 U.S.C. § 105(a)); *In re Diaz*, No. 8-14-bk-01237-CPM, 2014 WL 12936894, at *2–3 (Bankr. M.D. Fla. July 25, 2015) (issuing a *Martin-Trigona* Injunction pursuant to § 105(a) and other applicable statutes); *In re Smith*, No. 07-20244, 2012 WL 4758038 (Bankr. S.D. Ga. Sept. 17, 2012) (imposing pre-filing screening on the debtor continually filing groundless and frivolous litigation pursuant to 11 U.S.C. § 105(a) and the courts inherent powers); *In re Kozich*, 406 B.R. 949, 956 (Bankr. S.D. Fla. 2009) ("[I]n light of the broad authority I have under § 105 'to prevent an abuse of process,' as well as under my inherent power to control litigation conducted in bad faith, I find that the appropriate remedy is to prohibit [the debtor] from filing any adversary proceeding or contested matter in the United States Bankruptcy Court for the Southern District of Florida on a *pro se* basis without prior court approval"); *In re Mayhew*, No. 90-60141, 1994 WL 16006013, at

9

134

Hephzibah a/k/a Shekinah-El was afforded due process that her conduct may warrant sanctions.

A court must afford the party to be sanctioned due process in determining whether to issue sanctions.[28] Due process requires the party to have fair notice that her conduct may warrant sanctions, the reasons why, and an opportunity to respond.[29]

The Order to Show Cause provided Hephzibah a/k/a Shekinah-El with notice that the Court was considering invoking its authority to issue sanctions: "A Bankruptcy Court may [also] invoke its statutory power of [§] 105(a) to redress Rule 9011 violations, bad faith, and unreasonable, vexatious litigation."[30] The Court also put Hephzibah a/k/a Shekinah-El on notice of the sanctions it was contemplating and the specific conduct it considered sanctionable and vexatious:

> [T]he Court enters this Order to Show Cause to determine whether Hephzibah should be declared a vexatious litigant for (1) attempting to relitigate meritless and frivolous claims, (2) harassing Alleged Debtor, governmental agencies of the United States, and others, and (3) continuing to abuse the bankruptcy system.

---

*4 (Bankr. S.D. Ga. July 25, 1994) (imposing a pre-filing screening restriction on the debtor pursuant to the 28 U.S.C. § 1651(a) and 11 U.S.C. § 105(a)).

[28] *In re Mroz*, 65 F.3d at 1575 (citing *Chambers*, 501 U.S. at 49); *see also In re Evergreen*, 570 F.3d at 1273 ("Sanctions were also imposed under the bankruptcy court's inherent power which is similarly not affected by the safe harbor provision in Rule 9011.").

[29] *In re Mroz*, 65 F.3d at 1575 (citations omitted).

[30] Doc. 38, p. 10 (citations omitted).

10

135

The sanction this Court is considering, in addition to others that may result by virtue of prior orders entered in this case, includes permanently enjoining Hephzibah from initiating any matter or filing any papers in this Court (a) without prior approval from this Court or (b) unless she is represented by counsel admitted to practice in this Court. . . .

By filing the Involuntary Petition and other papers in this case with no apparent legal or factual basis, Hephzibah appears to have violated Rule 9011(b); she has clearly disregarded this Court's prior warnings against such conduct. If Hephzibah has any legal basis, facts, or evidence to show that this Involuntary Petition is not a repeat of her frivolous and vexatious filing history, she will have an opportunity to make her case at the hearing on this Order to Show Cause.[31]

CONCLUSION

As this Court again explained at the Order to Show Cause hearing, bankruptcy courts are not an appropriate forum for criminal matters, issues pertaining to alleged "international war crimes," or the other grievances for which Hephzibah a/k/a Shekinah-El seeks redress. The Involuntary Petition has nothing to do with bankruptcy whatsoever. The Involuntary Petition that commenced this case was filed in bad faith and for the sole purpose to harass; it was filed knowingly based on the same

---

[31] *Id.* at pp. 1–2, 13 (footnote omitted). Although the Order to Show Cause stated that sanctions may be issued pursuant to Rule 9011, the Court may still properly invoke its inherent authority because Hephzibah a/k/a Shekinah-El had notice of the specific conduct the Court considered sanctionable and vexatious. *See Fellheimer, Eichen & Braverman, P.C. v. Charter Techs., Inc.,* 57 F.3d 1215 (10th Cir. 1995).

11

136

"complaint" that had been dismissed with prejudice by another court. The record amply demonstrates that nothing short of an injunction will deter Hephzibah a/k/a Shekinah-El and those working with or through her from continuing to pursue additional frivolous and vexatious filings.[32] For that reason, it is appropriate to designate Hephzibah a/k/a Shekinah-El a vexatious litigant and impose sanctions.[33]

For the reasons stated, it is

ORDERED:

1. Pursuant to the Court's inherent authority and 11 U.S.C. § 105(a), Petitioning Party, Syteria Hephzibah, a/k/a Highly Favored Shekinah-El, and any anyone acting in concert with or at her behest, is permanently ENJOINED from initiating any matter or filing any papers in this Court without prior approval from this Court.

2. The following prescreening procedures shall apply:

   a. The Clerk's Office will not file any paper(s) or other document(s) tendered by Syteria Hephzibah, a/k/a Highly Favored Shekinah-El, and/or any anyone acting in concert or at her behest. Rather,

---

[32] See Silva, 2020 WL 5523400, at *12.
[33] See Gullet-El v. Corrigan, No. 3:17-cv-881-J-32JBT, 2017 WL 10861313 (M.D. Fla. Sept. 20, 2017).

12

137

any such papers will be date-stamped and delivered to Chambers to be reviewed and screened by the Bankruptcy Judge for the Northern District of Florida to determine whether the papers have arguable merit. No meritless, abusive, frivolous, scandalous, or otherwise impertinent filing shall be permitted. If the paper is arguably meritorious, the Court shall issue an order so stating and shall direct the Clerk of Court to file it accordingly.

b. In the event the Bankruptcy Judge's preliminary review determines that the proposed filing is frivolous, the papers tendered will not be filed with the Court. Instead, after making appropriate copies the Clerk will return the papers tendered to Hephzibah a/k/a Shekinah-El, or the original sender. Upon such a determination, Hephzibah a/k/a Shekinah-El will be subject to additional sanctions, including monetary assessment.

3. In addition to docketing this Order in the instant case, the Clerk shall open a miscellaneous case and shall file this Order in that case. Any order determining that a paper tendered by Hephzibah a/k/a Shekinah-El, and/or any anyone acting in concert or at her behest, has no arguable merit shall be filed in the miscellaneous

13

138

case, along with a copy of the paper in question; the Clerk shall then provide copies of both to the Office of the United States Trustee.

4. In the event that Hephzibah a/k/a Shekinah-El should appeal this Order, and in the further event that the District Court should hold that this Court does not have authority to issue this type of sanction, then this Order shall be construed as a Report and Recommendation (R&R) to the District Court.

5. In the event of any conflict between this Order and the Order entered in this case at Doc. 49., the terms of the instant Order shall control.

6. The Clerk's Office is directed to immediately re-close this case.

DONE and ORDERED on __January 22, 2021__.

KAREN K. SPECIE
Chief U. S. Bankruptcy Judge

cc: all parties in interest, including
Syteria Hephzibah
Highly Favored Shekinah-El
422 East 27th Street
Jacksonville, FL 32206-2211
dba Moorish Science Temple of America
dba Court of Equity and Truth

14

139

Citations

McIntyre, Catherine. "The Intriguing History and Controversy Surrounding the Moorish Science Temple of America." Broadview Magazine, March 21, 2022, https://broadview.org/moorish-science-temple-of-america-resurgence/

Carrot-Top Industries. "What Does the Gold Fringe on the American Flag Mean?" Carrot-Top Industries Blog https://www.carrot-top.com/blog/what-does-the-gold-fringe-on-the-american-flag-mean

U.S. Department of the Treasury. "Birth Certificate Bonds." TreasuryDirect.gov.https://www.treasurydirect.gov/laws-and-regulations/fraud/birth-certificate-bonds/

(Plotter Paper Guys. "What Projects Will Require the Use of Bond Paper?" Plotter Paper Guys, www.plotterpaperguys.com/what-projects-will-require-the-use-of-bond-paper/)

Municipal Association of South Carolina. "Handbook for Municipal Officials of South Carolina: Annexation and Incorporation."

https://www.masc.sc/sites/default/files/uploads/annexation-incorporation/incorp_handbook.pdf

Quora. https://www.quora.com/How-Do-I-Start-a-town-in-Texas#.~:text=How%20do%20I%20incorporate%20a,are%20resident%20in%20the%20community

"2024onlineshopru." Retrieved from https://2024onlineshop.ru/product/186113414133

Arab News."Riyadh Ardah: A Martial Dance Celebrates Kingdom's History, preserves its heritage." Arab News, https://www.arabnews.com/node/2375336/lifestyle

Wikipedia contributors."Order of King Abdulaziz." Wikipedia, The Free Encyclopedia. https://en.wikipedia.org/wiki/Order_of_King_Abdulaziz#The_Collar_of_Abdulaziz_Al_Saud

Made in the USA
Columbia, SC
15 February 2025

53898082R00080